CONGRESS
and the
CITIZEN-
SOLDIER

A publication of the Social Science Program
of the Mershon Center
for Education in National Security

CONGRESS
and the
CITIZEN-
SOLDIER

Legislative Policy-making
for
The Federal Armed Forces Reserve

By
WILLIAM F. LEVANTROSSER

OHIO STATE UNIVERSITY PRESS

For:

Verna
Susan
Nancy
Carol
and
Linda

PREFACE

EVER SINCE the founding of the American republic, the citizen-soldier has played a role in national security. The national military reserve of today, those forces exclusively under federal control, is the most recent edition of the revolutionary band of minutemen. In the last twenty years this federal reserve force has been solidly reinforced with legislative provisions of a rather permanent nature. This study attempts to document and analyze the role of Congress in developing policies for the reserve components of the armed forces during the past two decades.

My approach to this area of research has combined both historical and political analyses. I have chosen six major aspects of reserve affairs, perhaps the most crucial in the evolution of the modern reserve components and the most prominent from the standpoint of Congressional participation in reserve policy-making. The list is composed of the following: (1) retirement pay for reserve personnel based on inactive reserve training as well as active duty (Army and Air Force Vitalization and Retirement Equalization Act of 1948) ; (2) categories of readiness for reserve forces and obligations to serve in them (Armed Forces Reserve Act of 1952 and the Reserve Forces Act of 1955); (3) promotion criteria for reserve officers (Reserve Officer Personnel Act of 1954); (4) retention of paid-drill strength in the Army Reserve (Defense Appropriations Acts for Fiscal Years 1959-61); (5) officer recruitment on the college campus (ROTC Vitalization Act of 1964); and (6) realignment and reduction in strength of units in the Army reserve components (proposal to merge units of the Army Reserve into the National Guard in 1965).

Conclusions from this study have clustered around four major themes. First, Congressional primacy of interest in reserve affairs has been exceptional in comparison with the ascendancy of the executive branch in national defense policy-making. The maintenance of a relatively large number of drill-pay units and positions can be attributed in large measure to the support Congress has given to the citizen-soldier. Second, the Reserve Officers Association has emerged as an extremely effective interest group in sustaining programs for federal reservists in all components despite changes in defense strategy and military technology. In close liaison with Congressional leaders, it has been remarkably influential in building the federal military reserve. Third, elements of the legislative policy-making process have blurred the exercise of civilian control of the military. The political activities of citizen-soldiers have often encouraged professional military leaders to circumvent the policy proposed by civilian superiors. Fourth, the concept of the citizen-soldier has exhibited great durability by retaining its luster in the nuclear age. The reservist of today has been assigned greater responsibilities, but he has also been awarded some impressive benefits.

WILLIAM F. LEVANTROSSER

ACKNOWLEDGMENTS

I AM INDEBTED to many people for their help in this study. When they were at Wayne State University, Professors Samuel Halperin and Nicholas Masters encouraged me to begin a doctoral program, which eventually led to this area of research. At Rutgers, Professors Benjamin Baker, Ardath Burks, and Gerald Pomper offered guidance and experienced criticism which has greatly benefitted my writing.

Many individuals in both governmental and private organizations have given generously of their time for personal interviews. Without the benefit of their ability to provide insights, gained from years of dedicated service, this work would have lacked much of its understanding of armed forces reserve problems. To the many reservists who have provided me with camaraderie and a realistic perspective in reserve affairs, I also express my thanks.

The staff of the Rutgers University Library supplied a reference service of unsurpassed excellence. Mr. François-X. Grondin of the Government Documents section and Mr. Gilbert Kelley of the Reference Service left nothing to be desired in meeting my requests for materials.

My colleagues in the Mershon Social Science Program at the Ohio State University, led by the late Edgar S. Furniss, Jr., who was its director, served as stimulating catalytic agents in suggesting various ways in which I might approach the presentation of my research. The death of Professor Furniss as this work was about to go to press has removed a major source of inspiration for all those involved in the Mershon program; but I am confident that this inspiration will insure a continuation of the program as a living tribute to his work. His dedication to free inquiry and research in national security affairs and his personal manner will have a lifelong influence on me.

In the latter stages of preparing the manuscript for publication, two other individuals were most helpful. Professor Samuel P. Huntington, of Harvard University, read the entire manuscript and offered many helpful comments. Bernard Clorman completed the design for the book and the dust jacket. His artistic creativity and interest in the reserve program made a unique contribution to the final appearance of the book.

I would also like to acknowledge support in the form of a National Defense Graduate Fellowship, a Rutgers University Fellowship, and a Mershon Postdoctoral Fellowship, which permitted me to pursue my doctoral studies and to conduct this research on a full-time basis. I am also grateful for the generous leave policy of the public schools of Dearborn, Michigan.

To my wife and four daughters, already acknowledged in the dedication, I express my warm gratitude for foregoing many family pleasures so that I might devote time and energy to this study that otherwise might have been theirs. Their understanding is admirable.

Responsibility for errors in fact or interpretation is mine alone.

W. F. L.

August 22, 1966

CONTENTS

3   STATUS AND OBLIGATION — 51

4   PROMOTION AND PRECEDENCE — 75

5   RESERVE FORCE LEVELS — 97

9 CONCLUSIONS — 211

BIBLIOGRAPHY — 231

INDEX — 253

ILLUSTRATIONS

TABLES

1

SCOPE AND FOCUS OF STUDY
Development of Armed Forces Reserve Policy

1

SCOPE AND FOCUS OF STUDY
Development of Armed Forces Reserve Policy

SINCE THE END of World War I, an important source of military manpower has been the reserve components of the armed forces. Active programs of any consequence were not organized until after World War II, however. The Congress of the United States has maintained an active interest in these programs and has become closely involved in the development of policy for these reserve components. When judged from the standpoint of the small percentage of defense appropriations that go to reserve activities, the extent of Congressional participation in this aspect of national defense affairs has been unusual and disproportionately high.[1]

The constitutional authority of Congress to deal with policy-making for reserve forces is based on articles specifying its right to raise and support armies and navies, and to make rules regarding the regulation of the armed forces. Difficulty sometimes arises in the exercise of this authority because the grant of authority is not exclusive. In his constitutional role as commander-in-chief of the armed forces, the President also shares in the responsibility for developing policy for the military services. In recent years the Chief Executive through the defense establishment has become the initiator of policy proposals for the reserve components, while Congress has become extremely active in the role of reviewer and monitor. Whether by statute or by informal guidance to the executive departments, Congress can make clear its intent on policy without being responsible for the initiation of that policy. Although not all policy matters must be approved by, or be brought to the attention of, Congress, it is easy enough for Congress to bring any executive action under legislative scrutiny.

THE RESERVE COMPONENTS

In this study of policy-making for reserve forces, the emphasis is placed on those reserve components under exclusive federal control. Altogether there are seven reserve components, five of which are wholly federal in nature.[2] The Army and the Air Force each have two reserve components; both the Army National Guard and the Air National Guard are under state control during peacetime, although somewhere in the neighborhood of 90 per cent of their activities are financed by the federal government.[3] The governor through the state adjutant-general is guided by federal directives regarding training and administration of personnel in developing units for the dual mission of responding to state protective actions and to national emergencies. When National Guard units are called into federal service, state control ceases, and the units are then treated as other units in the active forces. In some cases they have been called to active duty to help enforce federal law within a state.[4]

The five reserve components under exclusive federal control have responsibilities to fulfil only on the national level, operating within their respective military services with the exception of the Coast Guard Reserve, which is controlled by the Treasury Department in peacetime. We shall be interested primarily in policy-making dealing with these five federal reserve components, but the two Guard components will be drawn in occasionally for attention because they are included in decisions for all reserve components. We shall not be concerned with decisions exclusively relevant to the National Guard.

Within the reserve components several classifications are used to designate the status of individuals. There is the three-category framework of Ready, Standby, and Retired Reserves based on susceptibility to recall to active duty. Those in the Ready group can be called to active duty by the President in time of national emergency, whereas the Standby and Retired groups may be called only by Congressional action.[5] Taking the Ready Reserve separately, we may, in turn, classify on the basis of remuneration received by the members. Those on a paid-drill status receive one day of base pay for each armory drill, or training session, of four hours duration (inactive duty training). It is possible to complete two armory drills in one day for which two days' pay is awarded. These reserve personnel also usually attend summer training for two weeks with the same pay that active forces receive. In some cases personnel will attend drills without pay but participate in two weeks of active duty training for pay. A few individuals will attend drills without pay and not go to any active duty training. In this case they will be in the Ready Reserve but on a completely non-pay status. Figures 1, 2, and 3 summarize the strengths of the various categories just enumerated.

In the United States the term "citizen-soldier" generally and loosely refers to any person affiliated with the service in a military capacity on a non-regular, non-professional basis. The hard-core of citizen-soldiers who may belong to interest groups and may work continually for reserve programs are those who have remained in the civilian components after

FIGURE 1*

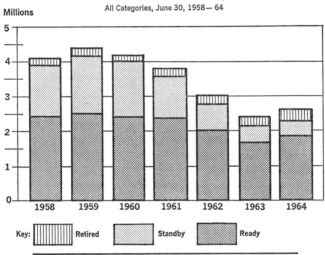

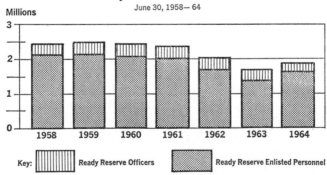

*U.S. Department of Defense, *Annual Report of the Secretary of Defense on Reserve Forces, Fiscal Year 1964* (Washington, D.C.: January 4, 1965), p. 64.

FIGURE 2*

Ready Reserves Not on Active Duty, by Component
June 30, 1961—64

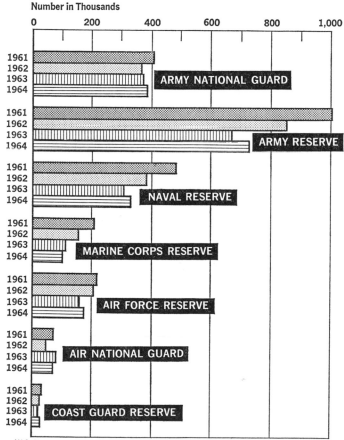

*U.S. Department of Defense, *Annual Report of the Secretary of Defense on Reserve Forces, Fiscal Year 1964* (Washington, D.C.: January 4, 1965), p. 66.

FIGURE 3*

Ready Reserves Resources, by Trained Status
June 30, 1960—64

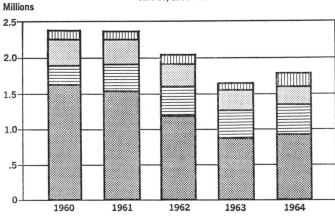

Reserves Actually in Paid Training, by Trained Status
June 30, 1960—64

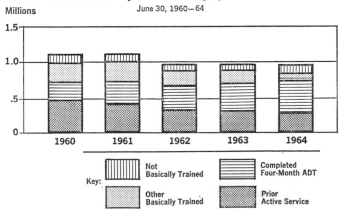

Key:

Not Basically Trained		Completed Four-Month ADT
Other Basically Trained		Prior Active Service

*U.S. Department of Defense, *Annual Report of the Secretary of Defense on Reserve Forces, Fiscal Year 1964* (Washington, D.C.: January 4, 1965), p. 69.

they have completed their obligated period of service. Those who have volunteered for reserve service as an alternative to being brought into the service through the draft would be considered candidates for the hard-core of citizen-soldiers while they are fulfilling their military obligation. The hard-core citizen-soldier would also be distinguished from the conscript in peacetime on the basis that the former serves over an extended period of twenty to thirty years, whereas the conscript is in the system for a relatively few years. In some countries the citizen-soldier may serve over a long period, but the service may not be in a voluntary status.[6]

Individual reservists may pass from a position in the reserve components to a position in the active forces. For example, an individual could leave a civilian role and volunteer for a tour of extended active duty for a prescribed number of years, perhaps three or four. Upon release from active duty, he would then return to a reserve component status. Some reserve officers have served full careers of twenty or more years of active duty without becoming regular officers. About one-sixth of the membership of the Reserve Officers Association is on extended active duty, a period in excess of ninety days.

The obligation to serve in a reserve component applies to everyone whether inducted, enlisted, or appointed in the armed forces prior to his becoming twenty-six years of age. The time spent by an individual in obligated service is distributed between active duty and inactive duty with the reserve components in various ways depending on the service and type of program involved, but the combination of active and inactive duty now required is a minimum of six years.[7] If an individual maintains his affiliation with a reserve component beyond the obligated time and continues to participate actively in the program, he may eventually qualify for retirement pay.[8] He also remains subject to recall to active duty regardless of family or occupational responsibilities.

NEED FOR THIS STUDY

Studies in national security affairs frequently omit analyses of the armed forces reserve components. It is hoped that this examination of the reserve components can fill that void to some extent. The evaluation of reserve forces has been an essential ingredient in military and diplomatic planning, and a significant number of civilians are engaged in reserve activities as part-time military personnel. In reserve policy-making we also see another aspect of executive-legislative relationships. Professional military personnel are involved in the process interacting with civilian directors and citizen-soldiers. In addition, interest groups actively representing both regular and reserve views in this area are sometimes accused of creating pressure to influence decisions not in the over-all best interests of the nation.

Each one of the above factors points to the need for an understanding of the process through which the national legislature contributes to the formulation of policy for the armed forces reserve components. Is there a well-delineated configuration of behavior that would establish a pattern in this field? What effect does national strategy have on manpower policy for the reserves? How good is the process in arriving at a solution to a defense problem within a democratic framework and without alienating professional military judgment or lessening the effectiveness of the program?

Although problems in the reserve area are not of the same magnitude as those involving nuclear weapons systems or expenditures for fulfilling foreign commitments, they are problems of national significance affecting both military requirements and over several million people directly. Members of reserve components are a link between defense officials and the public. Activities of reservists can be effective in influencing opinion on national defense affairs. Reservists, therefore, provide a network for widespread information dissemination, both geographically and occupationally.

There is also a need to devote attention to the role of Congress in reserve policy-making because twenty years of postwar developments in defense affairs now underline the fact that reserve strength levels are of more than a temporary nature. The politics of a large citizen-soldiery is a permanent feature of the government arena and ought to be so analyzed. At the same time there is a need to distinguish between the political processes involving the citizen-soldier and those values of the concept that may be considered apart from the political impact. In this study the emphasis is placed on the political processes, although assumptions will be made about the intrinsic value of the citizen-soldier in American life.

COMPARISONS WITH OTHER STUDIES

Some research has been conducted concerning the role of Congress in reserve forces policy-making, but it has tended to concentrate on National Guard affairs alone. A recent study on the political activity of the National Guard by Martha Derthick attempted to formulate same standards for judging the effectiveness of a political interest group by analyzing the actions of the National Guard Association. Dr. Derthick found that the success of the Guard was in large part the result of an environment within Congress conducive to favorable consideration of legislation for the National Guard.[9] There are, however, some significant differences between the Congressional approach to Guard proposals and to those for the exclusively federal reserve components. This study should help to make these differences clear and thus complete the picture of the Congressional role in policy-making for all reserve components.

Three other studies on the National Guard present various aspects of its history. William H. Riker followed the entire political life of the Guard and concluded that its success could be accurately described as an exchange of state autonomy for financial support.[10] A record of National Guard activities throughout its existence with primary attention given to battlefield achievements has just been completed by Jim Dan Hill.[11] The organization and mission of the Army National Guard has been covered in rather straightforward fashion by Chester Morrill.[12] In contrast, aside from the strictly federal approach, this study will focus on a somewhat shorter period of policy-making for the federal reserve components by limiting its analysis to the post-World War II era. It will not recount the battle experience of federal reserve units except insofar as it relates directly to Congressional consideration of policy for the federal reserve components.

There has been one investigation of federal reserve policy-making, but it was limited to the Army. Charles Dale Story presented an evaluation of policy for the two Army reserve components covering the first ten years after World War II. He concluded that interest group activity by the National Guard, the Reserve, and the professional military people endangered the objective evaluation of military requirements by pressing for goals to satisfy personal or professional interests rather than defense needs.[13] In comparison, this study will include policy-making for the federal reserve components for all services and cover a somewhat longer period by extending the analysis beyond 1957 to the present.

Other writings concentrating on either the legislative process or the substance of national defense policy have given only peripheral treatment to the reserve components.[14] It is the purpose of this study to focus on the legislative process as it directs its attention to policy for federal reserve forces. Only indirectly will the substance of that policy be considered, although certain assumptions will be made about it.

EARLY POLICY ON FEDERAL
RESERVE COMPONENTS

The tradition of civilians engaged in part-time military service has grown throughout America's history, but the life of reserve components of an exclusively federal nature has been relatively short. The reservist of the nuclear age continues in the tradition of the citizen-soldier and is asked to participate in training to a larger extent than ever before. In colonial America provision for community service as a part-time soldier to protect the settlement was a heritage from England. During the early days of the American republic, the development of state militia was an accommodation to the fear of a large standing army. Although President Washington had hoped for a well-organized militia established on a federal basis, the Militia Act of 1792 provided for a system of reserve forces under state control.[15] This system of using state military forces as the only national reserve for the Army prevailed until World War I.[16]

Reserve components under exclusive federal control, upon which this study focuses its major attention, were first authorized by legislation in 1916. The National Defense Act of June 3 provided the Army with a basis for organizing an Officers' Reserve Corps (ORC) and an Enlisted Reserve Corps (ERC), both with defined status in war and peace.[17] According to this statute, the Army of the United States was to consist of the Regular Army, the Volunteer Army, the ORC, the ERC, and the National Guard while in national service. The Act also conferred federal status on the National Guard; it was on this foundation that the Army has developed its two reserve components of today—the Army Reserve and the Army National Guard of the United States.[18] At the same time a Reserve Officers Training

Corps was authorized with senior divisions in colleges and special military schools, and junior divisions in high schools.

Reserve components for the Navy and Marine Corps were also initiated by law in 1916. Neither service, however, became seriously involved in the problems of handling a reserve component with both state and national status, as the Army did with the National Guard. The projected Naval Reserve Force was to constitute the main reserve capability, since the Naval Militia, a state force comparable to the Army National Guard, was maintained by only a few states.[19]

The demand for military manpower during World War I prevented full-scale development of these federal reserve components. The Naval Reserve Force expanded to 330,000 officers and men, while the Marine Corps Reserve grew to slightly over 6,000.[20] Some Army National Guardsmen were called as individuals to serve at the Mexican border in 1916, and this broke up many units. In 1917 Guardsmen were subject to the draft.

Policy for Army reserve components in the interwar period was adopted in the National Defense Act of 1920.[21] The three components of the Army were to consist of the Regular Army, the National Guard (while in the service of the United States), and the Organized Reserves (comprised of the Officers' Reserve Corps and the Enlisted Reserve Corps). The Guard remained essentially a state military force under state control, although it could become part of the Army of the United States when called to federal service. Reserve commissions for five years could be offered, and the graduates of ROTC soon began to receive most of these. Air Force personnel remained in either the Organized Reserve of the Army or the National Guard until 1947 when the Air Force was established as a separate military department. Just as the Army National Guard of the United States officially became a reserve component of the United

States Army in 1933,[22] the Air National Guard became a reserve component of the Air Force and bore the same relationship to the Air Force Reserve in the Air Force as the Army National Guard did to the Organized Reserve (Army Reserve) in the Army.[23]

Support for federal armed forces reserve programs in the twenties and thirties faced difficulties in the form of pacifist protests, isolationist sentiments, and economic depression. As the American Legion and the Reserve Officers Association urged a program of preparedness including more substantial aid to reserve forces, they exerted various forms of pressure on pacifist groups to prevent public demonstrations for the pacifist cause.[24] Appropriations for activities of the armed forces were reduced severely during the thirties. Despite these difficulties in securing support, the reserve components provided a substantial source of trained military manpower at the outset of World War II.[25] Reserve officers from all services numbered about 150,000 at that time.[26]

As the postwar era opened, the rapid demobilization of United States forces made the need for reserve forces more apparent. Guidelines for continued development of reserve forces in the Army had been issued in War Department Circular 347, dated August 24, 1944. General George C. Marshall as Chief of Staff brought his retired colleague, Brigadier General John McAuley Palmer, back to active duty specifically to formulate this document, which carefully outlined their ideas for a citizen army made up of a professional establishment no larger than necessary to meet normal peacetime requirements and a wartime army created from organized units in a citizen army reserve operating in time of peace.[27] The Palmer-Marshall program was strongly endorsed by President Truman, although the universal military service feature did not become an operating part of the program. Reserve components of the other services were also maintained. College ROTC programs trained officers for both the regular service and for the reserve components with the largest segment of the graduates finally settling in the reserve components after a period of active duty.

AREAS OF INVESTIGATION

The substantive areas of policy for the armed forces reserve selected for examination in this study serve as the vehicle for observing the role of Congress. These areas represent six major policy decisions in which Congress participated since World War II. Perhaps there are others that could have been included, but probably none could have displaced the selected policies in importance. They represent, as well, the full flavor of the reserve arena, and lead rather systematically to the policies of the present day. Although the emphasis is on the legislative process, it is difficult to divorce it from the substance of the policy itself. The range of substantive areas, as indicated below, seems adequate to permit an analysis of all the elements found in the legislative process dealing with reserve affairs.

One of the basic steps in establishing a permanent foundation for the postwar reserve program was the passage of the act providing retirement pay for reservists based partly on inactive duty training. Eligibility for retirement pay could be achieved with a minimum of twenty years of satisfactory service as a member of a civilian component of the armed forces. Service could consist of such activities as attendance at armory drills, completion of correspondence courses, and tours of active duty. The purpose of the legislation was to encourage reservists to make a long-term commitment to reserve service and thus provide an experienced force available in a national military emergency.[28]

Another important step in the formulation of postwar reserve policy was the Armed Forces Reserve Act of 1952. Ready, Standby, and Retired categories were to be used to classify reservists according to their susceptibility to recall to active duty.[29] Obligations to serve in these categories were further classified in the Reserve Forces Act of 1955 and can be considered together with the above act as a major reserve policy development.[30]

A prominent segment of the reserve program consists of officer personnel, and the Reserve Officer Personnel Act of 1954 provided criteria for judging the career development of reserve officers. Standards and procedures for promotion are specified on a basis somewhat parallel to those used for regular personnel.[31] The act as amended gives a permanent, long-range plan for the orderly development of an adequate supply of qualified officers in the reserve components.[32]

The fourth policy area deals with appropriations as a method of setting reserve policy. In the last three budgets proposed by the Eisenhower administration, attempts were made by the President to reduce the paid-drill strength of the two Army reserve components by cutting appropriations in that category by 10 per cent. Congressional action prevented this reduction and resulted in mandatory minimum strengths being written into appropriations acts.

Officer recruitment on the college campus is yet another area of concern for reserve policy-makers. The ROTC Vitalization Act of 1964 brought modifications in the approach of college training programs. With the incentive of scholarships for the students of the three services, defense leaders hoped to produce a greater supply of officers for the regular forces.[33]

The most recent major issue in the reserve policy area has been the proposal to merge the Army Reserve units into the National Guard to form a single Army reserve component. Congress blocked this proposal, but a Select Reserve Force was established in the Army made up primarily of National Guard personnel. In addition, over seven hundred units of the Army Reserve were disbanded. Consideration of this episode offers an opportunity to analyze present Congressional participation in reserve forces policy-making.

PATTERNS OF POSTWAR MILITARY POLICY

Each of the major aspects of reserve affairs of the post-war period studied here is related to the over-all pattern of United States military policy. Significant features of that policy may be sketched in broad strokes at this point as a framework of reference; these features can be covered later in greater detail as they become relevant in the analysis of each reserve policy issue. In this manner it should be possible to view reserve affairs in true perspective while looking carefully into the inner workings of legislative policy-making for the federal reserve components.

The outstanding feature of the postwar military policy has been the scope and depth of change stimulated by a hostile ideology and made possible by the application of technological advances. From a low point of demobilization in the late 1940's, the United States moved to a missile-spawning, nuclear bomb–laden stature requiring ever more sophisticated military personnel to wage war. The threats of communism brought forth a policy of containment applied to the Soviet Union in the cold war and tested on the battlefield in Korea, the latter bringing expansion of active forces through the recall to active duty of over 630,000 reservists in its first year. With the development of the H–bomb and the end of the Korean conflict, the New Look in military policy emphasized greater reliance on nuclear weapons and more support for reserve forces with an accompanying reduction in active military forces. Missiles, nuclear–propelled submarines, and nuclear warheads of various sizes constituted the new military hardware. Additional commitments were also assumed by the United States to nations throughout the world through participation in alliances intended to ring the Communist threats to the Free World. Finally, efforts were made in the late 1950's to trim the reserve components in size as part of a national strategy of massive retaliation.

A new administration in 1961 soon stopped talking about a missile gap and began building up active forces to meet the varied challenges of unconventional warfare in the jungles of Southeast Asia. By this time a strategy that foresaw time to mobilize and train forces after an emergency was declared now gave way to one that sought to establish a credible deterrent in a variety of packages tailored to provide a flexible response in a much quicker fashion. Increased attention was given to the readiness of reserve forces. Reaction and response times were reduced considerably. Looking at the reserve area some saw the need to transfer resources from reserve forces (i.e., reduce their numbers) to the active establishment while others thought the emphasis could be changed by maintaining a continuing high level of reserve forces and allocating additional resources to the active forces.

Policy for reserve forces is thus but one aspect of United States military policy. As attention is focused primarily on the reserve aspect in this study, it is not done with the intention of indicating that it is divorced from the rest of military policy. Nor is it to imply that developments in the reserve area can be explained completely within that area of military policy alone. However, once the broad framework is set for each policy issue in the reserve area, the major part of the analysis concentrates on the federal reserve components and delves deeply into the major decisions affecting them.

GOALS OF THIS STUDY

As the process of making reserve policy in each of these substantive areas is examined, the findings are arranged in three categories. The first deals with the nature of the role of Congress in making reserve policy. We are concerned with the scope of the issues, the approach of Congressional committees and their chairmen to problems in this area, the degree of public interest in the issues, the tension between the executive and legislative branches, and the framework within which the issues are stated. We are looking for evidence to support or refute the general proposition that Congressional primacy of interest in reserve affairs is exceptional in comparison with the ascendancy of the executive in national defense policy-making.

A second category concerns itself with the effects of Congressional action in the reserve policy area. Here the nature of civil-military relationships in a democratic nation becomes the focus of attention. The citizen-soldier fits into both civilian and military roles enjoying the citizen's privileges of full political participation without being restrained by some of the normal limitations applicable to professional military people. The status of the professional military person also becomes relevant in an evaluation of the degree of civilian control over the military in the policy process. The proposition under scrutiny here is one holding that the operation of civilian control over the military has been blurred but not endangered by elements of the process of reserve policy–making involving the legislature.

The third category of goals for this study includes the modes of political behavior of citizen-soldiers in the legislative arena. The organization and influence of interest groups dedicated to the concept of the citizen-soldier as embodied in the federal armed forces reserve will be carefully scrutinized. Comparisons will be made between the relationships of professional military people to Congress and the executive branch, and that of the citizen-soldier to the same groups. The major proposition in this category is that the politics of the citizen-soldier capitalizes on the acceptance of his movement back and forth between civilian and military spheres of activity when it is appropriate for his purposes.

ASSUMPTIONS

In the course of the analysis of the policy-making process on reserve affairs there are a few concepts I shall assume to be valid without attempting any lengthy documentation of them. The first regards the citizen-soldier. Given the nature of American commitments throughout the world and achievements of reserve personnel in World War II, it would be difficult to envision American military requirements' being filled without the use of the citizen-soldier, although the appropriate number might be debated. The arguments of John McAuley Palmer and George C. Marshall appear to be more relevant to national defense planning today than do the positions of Emory Upton or John C. Calhoun. A force composed entirely of regular troops as advocated by Upton would be too costly to maintain.[34] An expansible army as proposed by Calhoun would lack the expertise and leadership available among the hard-core citizen-soldier resources. Consequently, reserve forces manned by citizen-soldiers have become an essential ingredient in national security plans, and an understanding of the process through which policy for them is developed becomes an important factor in national defense evaluation.

Aside from the military and economic functions satisfied by the citizen-soldier there are additional reasons backing the validity of the concept. In such a vital activity as the common defense, it is a moral responsibility for citizens to share directly in the military duties required to be performed. If anything, the prospect of serving in a military role would make the general public more sensitive to the conditions that could move the nation closer to hostilities. In this way the citizen-soldier would help force an exacting appraisal of national security plans and help develop greater sensitivity to the implications of policies requiring the use of military force. To the extent that this phenomenon expands the participating citizenry in national decisions, it becomes a democratizing influence.

In a somewhat similar vein, it is hoped that an understanding of the manner in which policy for reserve forces is developed will enhance citizens' perceptions of what that policy should be. It might provide the basis for a more objective public evaluation of interest group positions. If enlightened policy is the result of broader understanding of the issues, then the principle of civilian affiliation with reserve forces will improve the democratic fabric of the nation.

The other assumption deals with the role of Congress in the formulation of policy for the armed forces. It would seem that if, in reserve affairs, Congress has exercised a significant share of authority in its partnership with the executive, this is an encouraging development. There may be factors in the reserve situation that naturally draw close Congressional attention and invoke a special brand of legislative concern. A recent symposium on the future of Congress produced the suggestion that if Congress cannot overcome the trends of insulation from the mainstream of America, of dispersion of political power within its body, and of large expenditures of time in oversight activity, it should abandon the legislative effort and focus upon the functions of constituent service and administrative control.[35] Perhaps the cases in policy-making for the reserve forces offer some insight into ways that Congress may avoid that fate.

As the first in a series of such cases, let us turn to the Act authorizing retirement pay for reserve personnel, which included credit for inactive duty service. This was one of the first policy enactments that determined the direction that reserve force development was to take in the postwar era.

Footnotes

1. About 2 per cent of the annual expenditures of the Department of Defense is assignable to reserve activities, although there are some minor expenses that are not separated from those of regular forces. This estimate was made on the basis of figures in the U.S. Treasury Department, Bureau of Accounts, *Combined Statement of Receipts, Expenditures and Balances of the United States Government for the Fiscal Year Ended June 30, 1964*, pp. 204–15, 223, 302–3.

2. 66 *Stat.* 481 (1952). Seven reserve components were established by the Armed Forces Reserve Act of 1952 as follows: National Guard of the United States, Army Reserve, Naval Reserve, Marine Corps Reserve, Air National Guard of the United States, Air Force Reserve, and Coast Guard Reserve.

3. Annual and biennial reports from the State Adjutants-General of Michigan, Montana, New York, Ohio, South Dakota, Vermont, and Washington for recent years.

4. The desegregation of Central High School at Little Rock, Arkansas in 1957 was accomplished with the federalization of the Arkansas National Guard after Governor Orval Faubus had attempted to prevent integration with the same troops under state control. At the University of Mississippi in September, 1962, federalized National Guard troops were used to maintain order during the registration of James H. Meredith, a Negro student. A year later public schools in Birmingham and three other Alabama cities were not desegregated until President John Kennedy federalized the National Guard to counter moves by Governor George C. Wallace to block desegregation.

5. 66 *Stat.* 481 (1952).

6. Such is the case in Switzerland, Sweden, and Israel. For a full account of comparative military manpower practices see M. R. D. Foot, *Men in Uniform* (New York: Frederick A. Praeger, 1961), pp. 64, 75, 78–9.

7. 77 *Stat.* 134 (1963).

8. 68 *Stat.* 1147 (1954); amended in 69 *Stat.* 218 (1955).

9. Martha Derthick, *The National Guard in Politics* (Cambridge, Mass., Harvard University Press, 1965), pp. 164–66.

10. William H. Riker, *Soldiers of the States* (Washington, D.C.: Public Affairs Press, 1957), p. 67.

11. Jim Dan Hill, *The Minute Man in Peace and War* (Harrisburg, Pa.: Stackpole Company, 1964).

12. Chester Morrill, "Mission and Organization of the Army National Guard of the United States: With Emphasis on the Period since 1952," (unpublished Ph.D. dissertation, American University, 1958).

13. Charles Dale Story, "The Formulation of Army Reserve Forces Policy: Its Setting amidst Pressure Group Activity," (unpublished Ph.D. dissertation, University of Oklahoma, 1958), pp. 267–68.

14. A small sampling of this category would include the following: Samuel Huntington, *The Common Defense* (New York: Columbia University Press, 1961); Jack Raymond, *Power at the Pentagon* (New York: Harper & Row, 1964); Tristram Coffin, *The Passion of the Hawks* (New York: Macmillan Co., 1964).

15. John K. Mahon, *The American Militia: Decade of Decision, 1789–1800* (Gainesville, Florida: University of Florida Press, 1960), pp. 14–24.

16. Riker, *op. cit.*, pp. 21–40.

17. 39 *Stat.* 189–95.

18. The Army National Guard has also retained a state role as a protective force to which it responds under control of the governors of each of the states while remaining bound to a federal call to duty; in this way the National Guard operates under a dual status.

19. 39 *Stat.* 587–93 (1916). The six classes in the Naval Reserve Force included the Fleet Naval Reserve, the Naval Reserve, the Naval Auxiliary Reserve, the Naval Coast Defense Reserve, the Naval Reserve Flying Corps, and the Volunteer Naval Reserve. The Naval Reserve was reorganized in 1925 and 1938 to operate with four main components: the Fleet Reserve, the Organized Reserve, the Volunteer Reserve, and the Merchant Marine Reserve.

20. House Committee on Armed Services, *History of United States Military Policy on Reserve Forces, 1775–1957*, Committee Paper No. 17, prepared by Eileen Galloway, 85th Cong., 1st sess., 1957, p. 457.

21. 41 *Stat.* 759 (1920).

22. 48 *Stat.* 153 (1933).

23. 61 *Stat.* 502 (1947); 63 *Stat.* 1016 (1949).

24. "Preparedness," *Reserve Officer*, IV (October, 1927), 20; William Gellermann, *The American Legion as Educator* (New York: Teachers College, Columbia University Press, 1938), pp. 180–86; and Marcus Duffield, *King Legion* (New York: Jonathan Capi & Harrison Smith, 1931), pp. 205–18.

25. Galloway, *op. cit.*, pp. 462–65.

26. Lee E. Sharff (ed.), *Uniformed Services Almanac*, 1964 (Washington, D.C.: Federal Employees' News Digest, 1964), p. 42.

27. Russell F. Weigley, *Towards an American Army* (New York: Columbia University Press, 1962), pp. 244–47.

28. 62 *Stat.* 1081 (1948).

29. 66 *Stat.* 481 (1952).

30. 69 *Stat.* 598 (1955).

31. 68 *Stat.* 1147 (1954).

32. 69 *Stat.* 218 (1955).

33. 78 *Stat.* 1063 (1964).

34. Active duty military personnel numbered 2.7 million at the end of June, 1963. Assuming that those in a paid reserve status are essential for United States military commitments and would be put on full-time duty according to Uptonian doctrine, approximately another million would be added to the total number of active military personnel. See note 6 *supra*.

35. Samuel P. Huntington, "Congressional Responses to the Twentieth Century," in David Truman (ed.), *The Congress and America's Future* (Englewood Cliffs, N.J.: Prentice-Hall, 1965), pp. 30–31.

2

RESERVE RETIREMENT PAY
Incentive for Long-term Commitment

2

RESERVE RETIREMENT PAY
Incentive for Long-term Commitment

ONE OF THE MAJOR STEPS in the development of the reserve components since World War II was the establishment of a non-disability retirement system. By offering an annuity to members of the reserve components, including the National Guard, this system provided an incentive for these members to make a long-term contribution to the reserve forces. Since this policy decision marked the acceptance of a new principle for the armed forces, an analysis of its formation should reveal important characteristics of the legislative policy-making process in reserve affairs.

The adoption of the principle of retirement pay for inactive duty, that is, for armory drills, occurred amid a flurry of activity in civilian component affairs. Decisions on this and other reserve forces policies at the time probably represented a turning point toward clear recognition of the importance of the reserve forces. It was the manifestation of a national estimate that military forces, including reserve components, would have to be kept at a higher peacetime level than ever before to meet the threats to peace posed by various Communist groups throughout the world. The reserve retirement plan paralleled the one given to regulars, and its consideration tended to revive the long-felt animosities between the reserve and the regular forces.

THE RESERVE ENVIRONMENT

In terms of interest to the members of the civilian components, the importance of retirement benefits was reflected in a survey by Representative Olin Teague of Texas. Inquiries were sent to the presidents of each state department in the Reserve Officers Association requesting suggested priorities for legislative action on reserve matters. Top priority was assigned to the retirement proposal by 38 per cent of the departments.[1]

There were certain postwar conditions directly affecting the outcome of a decision on a retirement plan for the reserve forces. In the wake of rapid demobilization, attitudes of resistance to further association with military activities developed. Pressures for veterans' bonuses produced successful results in many states but not at the federal level. Criticism arose over the action to release those who had served in the war from the reserve obligations contained in Section 3c of the Selective Service Act of 1940.[2] Proposals for universal military service to secure a group from which trained reservists could be developed failed to find favor in Congress despite the urging of the War Department and the President. It also became apparent that if the United States were to exercise a position of leadership in the world, a higher level of military forces than ever before, both regular and reserve types, had to be kept available in peacetime. The concern with a position of international leadership also weighed heavily in the face of growing disenchantment with the policies of the Soviet

Union toward the United States and other Western nations. If military might was necessary to meet Soviet expansion, then a source of military strength found in the reserve components should become a concern of policy-makers. Major changes also occurred during this early postwar period in the organization of governmental bodies and agencies dealing with military problems. In Congress an armed services committee in each house began to handle military policies for all services starting in 1947 under the provisions of the Legislative Reorganization Act of the previous year. At about the same time a National Military Establishment was founded in an attempt to unify the entire defense structure of the nation. Intensified inter-service rivalry was one of the initial results of the military reorganization under the Department of Defense. Efforts to reduce this rivalry included proposals to standardize procedures for the three service departments in such personnel matters as retirement plans.

Simmering antagonism between regulars and the reserve components, especially in the Army, accompanied the legislative deliberations on the retirement plan for civilian components. At times it appeared that this feeling was almost deliberately invoked by military associations seeking to stimulate or unify their own membership. Numerous examples of this feeling exist in the proceedings and communications of the National Guard Association and the Reserve Officers Association.[3] Both blamed the professionals' errors in judgment made in planning for the poor military posture, and they accused the regular forces of trying to get rid of civilian component personnel. Public recognition of the hostility that could be fanned between the civilian components and the regulars was acknowledged indirectly by the issuance of a directive by the Army Chief of Staff early in 1948 that was designed to promote better relations between the various components of the Army.[4]

Military associations such as the National Guard Association and the Reserve Officers Association were busy during the early post–World War II period restoring their organizations to working order and focusing attention on the need to maintain higher reserve force levels after the demobilization letdown. Brigadier General E. A. Evans was given a special release from active duty and his duties on the General Staff Committee on Reserve Policy at the request of the ROA in order that he might assume the civilian position of executive director of that organization. In June, 1946, just before its first postwar convention, the ROA had a rapidly increasing membership of slightly over 100,000.[5] The National Guard Association, with a rising strength of about 70,000, was active under the leadership of Major General Ellard Walsh, who worked closely with Major General Milton A. Reckord, President of the Adjutants General Association.[6] Each of these military associations had adopted resolutions at their national meetings supporting legislative action for a retirement system for civilian component personnel with credit for inactive duty training as a means of stimulating reserve personnel to participate in unit training.

THE PRINCIPLE OF RESERVE RETIREMENT

Until 1946 the War Department had opposed all proposals that would authorize retirement pay for reserve personnel if it were computed on the basis of time spent on inactive duty training.[7] Although a man had undergone training at an evening or a weekend drill, this activity should not be credited toward retirement benefits according to the War Department. Presumably, training during active duty for two weeks during the summer was acceptable, since it was on a full-time status.

The proponents of the reserve retirement plan claimed many advantages for it. Wanting to have a strong reserve and to protect it against the high turnover experienced between world wars, Congressman Overton Brooks regarded non-disability retirement pay for civilian components as an incentive for qualified reserve personnel to remain active over a long period.[8] Since veterans with important skills were still available from World War II, this was a critical time for instituting such a program. Considerable controversy existed concerning the gap between the War Department's declared policy of support for a large active reserve and its implementation during the first two or three years after World War II. Before the end of World War II, General George C. Marshall as Army Chief of Staff had approved plans granting a prominent place to citizen-soldiers in future security forces, but fulfilment of the plans was very slow.[9]

Although Navy reservists and National Guardsmen had been getting pay for training drills, even a proposed drill pay provision for all services was not regarded as sufficient lure for the quality personnel that would be attracted by a retirement program.[10] Requirements to qualify for retirement benefits were to be so established that previous service could be counted, and thus some reward would be given for service completed before the passage of the legislation. A strong, stable reserve force with experience and youth was the goal.

FIRST LEGISLATIVE ATTEMPT

The first serious legislative consideration of non-disability retirement benefits for civilian components came in the second session of the Seventy-ninth Congress. Bills introduced for the War Department in both houses of Congress contained sections on the elimination of ineffective regular officers and on the rank to be used by regular personnel in establishing retirement compensation in addition to a retirement system for reserve officers. The measure introduced by Senator Burnet Maybank in March, 1946, would have required fifteen years of active service by reservists to qualify for any retirement pay. At that point the War Department opposed the extension of retirement benefits to reserve personnel for inactive duty training. When the representatives of the various military and veterans' groups were summoned for the Senate hearing without advance notice of the proposals, they requested time to study them.[11] It was clear that the War Department had not consulted with either the General Staff Committee's Advisory Section on Civilian Components or the various interested military associations.[12] At the next hearing, during the first week of April, considerable opposition to War Department provisions in the bill was offered by the military associations.

Subsequently, conferences were held between the Secretary of War, the Army Chief of Staff, and representatives of the Reserve Officers Association and the National Guard Association to arrive at some proposal on retirement benefits for civilian components that would be acceptable to all groups. Finally, in July, 1946, the War Department gave its approval to the principle of granting retirement credit for inactive duty training.[13] This was a real breakthrough for the civilian components.[14]

During this period of conferences and hearings in 1946, requests for support from the President were channeled through his military aide, Major General Harry H. Vaughn. The latter announced that retirement benefits for inactive duty *would* be in accord with the President's program, contrary to announcements from the Bureau of the Budget.[15] It was further understood that the military associations would not oppose a three-year minimum of active duty as a requirement to qualify for reserve retirement assuming that the passage of a universal military training bill would provide sufficient opportunities for active duty time to fulfil such a requirement.

These provisions were embodied in H.R. 7063, which came before the House sitting as the Committee of the Whole on July 26, 1946. At this time the bill applied only to the Army and proposed that the Veterans Administration function as a certification agent for the disbursal of retirement pay. With the expressed support of General of the Army Dwight D. Eisenhower as Army Chief of Staff, the bill passed on a unanimous consent basis.[16]

Before the Senate a somewhat similar version of the bill was passed over. Senators Edwin Johnson of Colorado and Lister Hill of Alabama objected to unanimous consent on the grounds that the House version, which they felt would give too much reward for past service, might prevail in the conference committee.

Although evidence from hearings and organization magazines indicated that the military associations and the veterans' groups worked together very closely on the issue, events sometimes moved faster than these organizations could follow with effective support. The executive director of the Reserve Officers Association indicated that it was important to the success of some bills for state departments and local chapters to respond promptly with messages of support to congressmen when asked to do so by the professional staff of the association seeking to fulfil organization mandates.[17] In 1946 it was probably expecting too much for many chapters to respond promptly when they were just being reconstituted for the first full year of operation after the war. They could not always muster the type of grass-roots support that congressmen like to see. In some cases there was even an expression of sentiment from local chapters of ROA that conflicted with, or questioned the national position of, the organization. The national staff worked on the assumption that getting a bill passed establishing the principle of reserve retirement was more important than trying to secure a satisfactory measure in every detail. Communications from ROA national headquarters to state and local units did not make the goal clear, however, and Congress got the idea that the federal reserve components did not know what they wanted.

THE EIGHTIETH CONGRESS TAKES OVER

Although the Seventy-ninth Congress failed to enact reserve retirement legislation, pressure continued to build up in 1947 from the National Guard Association and the Reserve Officers Association for a comprehensive retirement plan that would include Army Reserve and National Guard eligibility. In the previous year the War Department had joined the Navy and military reserve associations in supporting non-disability retirement benefits for civilian components. However, the War Department was primarily interested in titles of the bill dealing with elimination of ineffective regular officers and rank designations for regular retirement pay.

The efforts of reservists were also spurred on by military commentators wondering about the future of reserve forces. Charges that perhaps the Army did not really want the reserve components because so little was being accomplished in providing for them aroused reservists to work even harder for retirement legislation.[18] The reaction continued even after Secretary of the Army Robert P. Patterson made the affirmation that the War Department really did want the reserve forces.[19]

The Eightieth Congress, controlled by the Republicans and operating under the Legislative Reorganization Act of 1946, began work, in revised committees, on another measure incorporating the idea of non-disability retirement benefits for inactive duty training and establishment of an incentive for participation in reserve training. H.R. 2744, as originally introduced by Overton Brooks in March, 1947, included three titles. The first and second dealt with elimination and retirement of regular Army officers. The third title provided for non-disability retirement benefits for qualified personnel of the reserve components of all the services.

The retirement system proposed in H.R. 2744 granted retirement pay at age sixty to those who had completed a minimum of twenty years of satisfactory service. A satisfactory year was one in which fifty or more retirement points had been earned. A drill meeting or a day of active duty was each worth one point, for example. The minimum active duty requirement to establish eligibility was six months. The retirement pay was to be computed on the basis of the points earned and the rank achieved.[20] The Administrator of Veterans' Affairs was to act as disbursing agent. This was the broad outline of the bill as it started through the legislative process of the first session of the Eightieth Congress.

Prior to the hearings on H.R. 2744 in the House, representatives of the major military associations and veterans' groups had met with military and civilian officials of the War Department and had agreed to most of the provisions that were to be included in the bill. There is some indication that the Army Chief of Staff, General Eisenhower, suggested that the provisions for regular officers be placed in a separate bill, but spokesmen for both the National Guard Association and the Reserve Officers Association successfully opposed the move.[21] One item on which agreement could not be secured in advance of the hearings concerned the designation of a disbursing agent for the retirement pay. The War Department wanted to designate the

Veterans Administration, but that agency requested that the services handle that role just as they did with regular retirement. Opposition to this proposal also came from veterans' groups such as the Veterans of Foreign Wars, who felt that responsibility for disbursing funds in this area might endanger appropriations for veterans' programs and that association of the Veterans Administration with the bill would tend to put a "pension" label on it.[22] Although general agreement appeared among the interested parties on the retirement provisions as well as the other two titles of the bill in the hearings, H.R. 2744 failed to get floor action after being reported by the Armed Services Committee.

Before the second session of the Eightieth Congress began, the coalition of support for the bill ran serious risks of dissolution. Major General Harry H. Vaughn proposed a merger of the Army National Guard and the Army Reserve under federal control.[23] This followed in the spirit of unification promoted by the formation of a single National Military Establishment and the installation of James Forrestal as the first Secretary of Defense in September of 1947. Although the National Guard violently objected to a merger with the Army Reserve, the ROA and the War Department favored the proposal. From time to time discussion of the merger proposal strained relations of the National Guard Association with the Reserve Officers Association and the Pentagon.

Another source of alienation between the Reserve Officers Association and the National Guard Association was the feeling that the postwar organization of the Guard would be completed before major attention was given to the Army Reserve.[24] In his appearance before the Gray Board, Brigadier General Evans, Executive Director of the ROA, made it clear that both reserve components of the Army ought to proceed abreast in developing a balanced reserve force.[25] Perhaps a greater danger to the harmony of the parties supporting the reserve retirement principle was the evidence of lower priority treatment for the reserves by the Department of the Army that aroused reserve attacks of a rather broad nature on the Regular Army. The legislative adviser for the ROA indicated that regulars were unappreciative of the efforts of the reservists and were attempting to get the support of the ROA, "while offering only crumbs in return."[26] Although these dangers to the coalition of support for reserve retirement legislation existed, they never caused a dissolution of the coalition.

At the highest level, relations between the ROA and the national military leaders appeared good. Secretary of Defense James Forrestal accepted the post of Honorary National Chairman of the ROA-sponsored National Security Week observance in February, 1948.[27] When General Omar Bradley replaced General Eisenhower as Army Chief of Staff, no change in the previously favorable Army position on reserve retirement was indicated.

In the Congressional hearings, professional military men of the separate services and the officials of the executive branch acknowledged the co-ordinating role of the Bureau of the Budget by stating whether their remarks had the prior approval of the Bureau. In addition to granting clearances on statements on the reserve retirement act, the Bureau of the Budget in an unprecedented action requested the House in early 1948 to withhold action on H.R. 2744, which had been favorably reported in the first session of the Eightieth Congress, until the Gray Board had made its report.[28] However, the request was not honored, and the bill passed the House on March 10, 1948.

In the hearings on the other side of the Capitol, Senator Harry Byrd of Virginia examined H.R. 2744 closely from the standpoint of costs, but these considerations never seriously endangered the chances of the bill. Since the actuarial estimates rested on such assumptions as the number of personnel yet to come into the service and the requirements of national security, the range of cost estimates for the retirement provision was great. The most commonly cited figure was a peak of $18 million for reserve retirement pay in 1963.[29] Current practice in reporting on expenditures does not distinguish between regular and reserve retirement costs, so the accuracy of the earlier estimate cannot be checked.[30]

Testimony at the Senate hearings in 1948 also revealed that any ill will that existed between the military services and the military associations or between the military associations themselves had subsided. A letter from Secretary of Defense Forrestal to the Senate Armed Services Committee endorsed the Senate version of Title III in H.R. 2744 dealing with reserve retirement.[31] Indirectly it was also indicated that the Gray Board concurred in the Secretary's endorsement. With success for a reserve retirement system then in sight, the National Guard Association and the Reserve Officers Association worked together in support of the Senate version of the bill.

The Senate revision of H.R. 2744 differed from the House reserve retirement provisions by removing the active duty requirement for eligibility and by simplifying the method of computing retirement pay. The only active duty requirement remaining was the annual two-week tour of summer field training for those personnel earning points through participation in an active drill unit. Instead of one retirement pay rate for active duty credit and another for inactive duty credit, a single rate of 2.5 per cent was established. When this rate was used in conjunction with the base pay of the highest rank attained and the total points earned, the retirement pay due at age sixty could be computed but the final amount could not exceed 75 per cent of the active duty pay. Each service, rather than the

Veterans Administration, was required to establish implementing regulations and to arrange for the disbursal of retirement pay.[32] In this form, Title III became part of H.R. 2744 as it was passed by the Senate.[33] The House concurred with the Senate version of the bill and sent it on to the President, who signed it into law on June 29, 1948.

For President Truman the appeal of the reserve retirement section was evidently so strong that his statement upon signing the bill was confined to that part of the law.[34] His close association with National Guard and Reserve activities in an earlier period was evident in his approach to military reserve problems.[35] In his statement of praise for the reserve retirement provisions in the law, he emphasized the need for teamwork between all components of the services in order to develop an effective national defense force.

ANALYSIS OF THE PROCESS

A major element in the analysis of the legislative process as it deals with reserve forces policy is the type of proposal under consideration by Congress. Although an incentive program for reservists could be responsible for retention of a significant number of reservists as a reservoir of military personnel required for national security, the procedure for handling the establishment of a retirement program for reservists was accomplished within the framework of domestic politics. In the case of the retirement system for reserve forces personnel, the proposal was rather narrow in scope. It was neither a matter of great public interest nor was it one that seriously threatened any particular group. Consequently, national legislators were relatively free to follow their own convictions, perhaps those of a colleague on a committee examining the proposal, or the counsel of interest groups. Provisions of the Vitalization and Retirement Equalization Act were somewhat technical and detailed, and national legislators were inclined to follow the recommendations of committee members who had developed specialized knowledge in this area of legislation. In this way, the influence of the House and Senate Armed Services committees was expanded. At the same time the need for competent information on the impact of the provisions in the act gave military associations interested in its passage, such as the National Guard Association and the Reserve Officers Association, an opportunity to counsel with the legislators.

With a narrower scope and fewer interest groups participating than in other types of legislation, a greater premium was placed on the ability of each interest group to formulate the specific provisions of the bill for a reserve retirement system. The ROA and the NGA worked closely with professional military leaders because all three groups had something at stake in the bill. The chief restraining force was the Bureau of the Budget, but it was effectively held in check by the President. Civilian heads of the three military service departments accepted professional military recommendations. At this time the Secretary of Defense had not developed strong control over the separate services and probably could not have effectively blocked their proposals if he had opposed them. In this case, however, he did concur with the position taken by the separate services.

Another significant feature of the legislative process in the reserve retirement matter was the ease of access to the War Department meetings for the military associations when proposals were being formulated for Congressional action. At conferences prior to the hearings, these interest groups were able to forge a consensus for support of their proposals. Any differences were ironed out even before public hearings took place. In this manner the way was smoothed for favorable Congressional action. President Truman's close bond with reserve activities throughout his life also made it possible for the ROA and the NGA to gain his sympathetic attention. That it was an election year gave the President yet another reason to act on behalf of the reserve components. On this issue the President overruled objections from the Bureau of the Budget based on the future cost of the retirement system.

The ROA and the NGA did not take the endorsement of a retirement plan for reserve forces by the professional military leaders as any assurance of success, since both aroused their members to gain support for the retirement legislation. Reserve suspicion of long-range professional military goals, which might not include reserve forces, had not completely subsided. Probably enough of this feeling remained among reservists to maintain the internal cohesion required to sustain a successful effort.

As the retirement system for reservists went through the legislative process, partisanship was not a relevant influence. The Army and Air Force Vitalization and Retirement Equalization Act had bipartisan support when it was passed by the Republican-controlled Eightieth Congress. Success was not due to change in party control of Congress but rather to changing world conditions and to more effective interest group activity. Military affairs in the legislative process have usually transcended partisan and sectional differences, and this is especially true of issues affecting the reserve forces.

The reserve retirement system was a major breakthrough for the reserve forces. For its part in the achievement, the ROA took its place beside the NGA as one of the most effective military associations dealing with reserve affairs in the legislative process. As other reserve affairs came before Congress, the ROA was to take an increasingly effective part in influencing their outcome.

An important implication of the reserve retirement system for the political process was that it established vested interests in future military legislation dealing with civilian

TABLE 1

GUIDE FOR ESTIMATING MONTHLY RETIREMENT PAY IN THE RESERVE COMPONENT*

RANK OR PAY GRADE	15 YEARS INACTIVE DUTY AND 5 YEARS ACTIVE DUTY	25 YEARS INACTIVE DUTY AND 5 YEARS ACTIVE DUTY	20 YEARS INACTIVE DUTY AND 3 YEARS ACTIVE DUTY
COMMISSIONED			
0-8 Major General	$265.32	$410.03	$224.49
0-7 Brigadier General	238.85	356.61	195.25
0-6 Colonel	183.56	313.32	158.10
0-5 Lieutenant Colonel	165.67	255.52	139.90
0-4 Major	143.72	213.66	116.98
WARRANT			
W-4 Chief Warrant Officer	119.42	197.72	100.40
ENLISTED			
E-9 Sergeant Major	98.62	168.27	84.46
E-8 Master Sergeant	86.44	150.62	74.51
E-7 Sergeant 1/Class	76.25	135.09	66.22
E-6 Staff Sergeant	67.14	99.82	54.64
E-5 Sergeant	56.95	84.67	46.36

*Based on pay rates effective in 1966. Each member must compute his pay individually since his credit varies slightly from that of another, but the above figures suggest some appropriate ranges. Monthly payments begin at age sixty.

components of the armed forces for all potential recipients of the benefits. Such a condition created the possibility that interest groups would seek more and more statutory provisions favorable to them. One staff member of the House Armed Services Committee at the time was so opposed to the reserve retirement pay that he asked to be kept off the subcommittee work dealing with the proposed legislation. He pictured waves of reservists raiding the Treasury.[36]

Perhaps the range of reserve retirement pay can best be determined by reference to Table 1. Lower ranks in officer and enlisted categories are not given because it is quite likely that persons with at least twenty years of service would have reached the steps listed. It is also assumed that the inactive duty service would include the equivalent of weekly participation in drills and two weeks' summer training. Not only are reservists interested in the retirement pay, but they also follow action on appropriations to support the facilities and personnel necessary to provide conditions for earning points to qualify for the retirement pay.

Provision of retirement benefits for inactive duty training was a major step in the building of the reserve components. It offered the basis for some stability in reserve forces planning. It came in the same year as other major provisions for the reserve forces, such as drill pay for the Reserves of the Army and the Air Force and an executive order to strengthen the reserve components. It passed with the co-operation of the major military associations and veterans' groups. It offered some hope for a lessening of the animosity between regulars and reservists, particularly in the Army.

Both the principle of reserve retirement and the tangible benefits coming from it were important in the development of the postwar reserve program. Acceptance of the principle raised the status of reservists because it meant participation in a retirement system with professional military personnel. Hope of earning eligibility for monetary payments in later life became an influence in the retention of experienced reservists in a long-term program.

With legislation on reserve retirement completed, attention now shifted to other affairs of the reserve forces. Mobilization experience in the Korean conflict stimulated legislative review of their organization and administration. The Reserve Acts of 1952 and 1955 focused on problems in these areas, and we shall now turn to these two legislative policy decisions.

Footnotes

1. "A Congressman Inquires," *Reserve Officer*, XXV (May, 1948), 16, 23.

2. "The President's Report," *Reserve Officer*, XXV (May, 1948), 17. This section specified assignment to a reserve component for ten years or until age forty-five, whichever came sooner, but it was never implemented.

3. "Annual Report of the President," *Official Proceedings of the National Guard Association of the United States*, Sixty-sixth Annual Convention, 1944, p. 86. William H. Neblett, "The President's Report," *Reserve Officer*, XXIV (October, 1947), 23.

4. Marion B. Richardson, "Let's Get Practical," *Reserve Officer*, XXV (April, 1948), 10.

5. *Reserve Officer*, XXIII (June, 1946), 21.

6. House Committee on Armed Services, *Subcommittee Hearings on H.R. 2744*, Committee Paper No. 169, 80th Cong., 1st sess., 1947, p. 3372.

7. Senate Committee on Military Affairs, *Hearings, Retirement*, S. 1974, 79th Cong., 2d sess., 1946, p. 3.

8. *Congressional Record*, 80th Cong., 2d sess., 1948, p. 2487. The turnover rate for Army reserve officers between world wars was 10 per cent annually. Congressman Brooks had been working for reserve retirement pay since 1941.

9. *The War Reports of General of the Army George C. Marshall, General of the Army H. H. Arnold, and Fleet Admiral Ernest King* (New York: J. B. Lippincott Co., 1947), pp. 295–99. War Department Circular 347, issued in August, 1944, also declares this position.

10. Drill pay for Army and Air Force reserve personnel was authorized shortly before the retirement bill was passed (62 *Stat.* 157 [1948]). The drill pay bill passed the Senate in 1947, and it was approved in the House in 1948 by a unanimous voice vote. (*Congressional Quarterly Almanac*, IX [1948], 244–45).

11. Senate Committee on Military Affairs, *Hearings, Retirement*, S. 1974, 79th Cong., 2d sess., 1946, p. 15.

12. *Ibid.*, p. 25. The ROA emphasized the high ratio of reserve officers to regular officers in World War II—835,000 to 15,000—as an indication that some attention should be given to their interests. Contention over the value of each group is probably one of the underlying reasons for the antagonism between regulars and reservists throughout the immediate postwar period.

13. House Committee on Military Affairs, *Hearings on H.R. 6954, H.R. 7063 and Other Bills Relating to Retirement*, 79th Cong., 2d sess., 1946, p. 41.

14. The regulars undoubtedly hoped that this would improve the chances for the entire bill, which included provisions for regular retirement and elimination of ineffective officers.

15. Senate Committee on Military Affairs, *Hearings, Retirement*, S. 1974, 79th Cong., 2d sess., 1946, p. 57.

16. *Congressional Record*, 79th Cong., 2d sess., 1946, p. 10178.

17. *Reserve Officer*, XXIII (September, 1946), 17–18.

18. *Ibid.*, XXIV (May, 1947), 24.

19. *Ibid.*, XXIV (July, 1947), 12–13.

20. House Committee on Armed Services, *Subcommittee Hearings on H.R. 2744*, Committee Paper No. 169, 80th Cong., 1st sess., 1947, pp. 3293–99.

21. *Ibid.*, pp. 3365, 3479. Major General Melvin Maas, representing the Reserve Officers Association, the Marine Corps Reserve Officers Association, the Military Order of the World Wars, and the Reserve Officers of the Naval Service, presented the idea most colorfully when he said, "But we have learned from practice that when we want a ride, we hitchhike."

22. *Ibid.*, p. 3559.

23. *New York Times*, October 2, 1947, p. 26.

24. House Committee on Armed Services, *Subcommittee Hearings on H.R. 2744*, Committee Paper No. 169, 80th Cong., 1st sess., 1947, p. 3633.

25. *Army and Navy Journal*, LXXXV (February 14, 1948), 627. Specifically, he charged that one of the greatest difficulties facing the Organized Reserve was the policy of the Department of the Army of holding back action on Reserve matters until the completion of the National Guard program. The Committee on Civilian Components, appointed by the President and headed by Gordon Gray (Gray Board), agreed with General Vaughn's proposal, but its findings were not made public until after the reserve retirement bill had been passed. However, testimony before the Gray Board was released in 1948 as the retirement bill was being considered by Congress.

26. John P. Oliver, "Legislation in the 80th Congress," *Reserve Officer*, XXV (January, 1948), 12.

27. *Army and Navy Journal*, LXXXV (January 10, 1948), 485.

28. *Congressional Record*, 80th Cong., 2d sess., 1948, p. 2481.

29. Senate Committee on Armed Services, *Hearings, Army and Air Force Vitalization and Retirement Equalization Act of 1948*, H.R. 2744, 80th Cong., 2d sess., 1948, p. 28.

30. Treasury Department, *Combined Statement of Receipts, Expenditures and Balances of the U.S. Government for the Fiscal Year Ended June 30, 1963*, pp. 214–15.

31. Senate Committee on Armed Services, *Hearings, Army and Air Force Vitalization and Retirement Equalization Act of 1948*, H.R. 2744, 80th Cong., 2d sess., 1948, p. 13.

32. Senate Committee on Armed Services, *Providing for Elimination of Regular Army and Air Force Officers*, S. Rept. 1543 to accompany H.R. 2744, 80th Cong., 2d sess., 1948, p. 9.

33. *Congressional Record*, 80th Cong., 2d sess., 1948, p. 7713.

34. *New York Times*, June 30, 1948, p. 21.

35. Harry S Truman, *Memoires, I, Year of Decisions* (Garden City, N.Y.: Doubleday and Co., 1955), pp. 128, 138–39. President Truman served with the Missouri National Guard in World War I. Later he organized Army, Navy, and Marine Corps reserve officers in the greater Kansas City area in 1921 into ROA Chapter No. 1, and he was elected president of that group.

36. Interview with Mr. Bryce N. Harlow in Washington, D.C., on May 27, 1964. Mr. Harlow later served as a presidential assistant throughout the entire Eisenhower administration. Although his duties were primarily in writing, he was frequently asked to advise on armed forces reserve matters.

3

STATUS AND OBLIGATION
Reserve Acts of 1952 and 1955

3

STATUS AND OBLIGATION
Reserve Acts of 1952 and 1955

WHATEVER PRESSURE was needed to initiate a revision of armed forces reserve manpower policies was supplied by the demands of large-scale American participation in the Korean conflict.[1] In strategic terms the action in Korea was a major test of the containment policy. Perhaps the major complication was that American involvement was not great enough to require full mobilization of military manpower. The lack of a uniform organization of reserve forces and the absence of a sound understanding of emergency obligations on the part of reservists created problems for those attempting to field a force required by national security policy. An analysis of the development of the legislative policies embodied in the Reserve Acts of 1952 and 1955 will reveal the process through which solutions to these problems were sought.[2]

THE PROBLEMS

Immediate military manpower requirements for Korea were met with units of the regular forces supplemented by reservists called back to active duty. However, since this mobilization of reservists was only partial, the need was largely for individual enlisted men and junior officers from reserve pools. What was not generally understood was that unit integrity of the reserve components had to be maintained for missions during full mobilization. To many it seemed that reserve units receiving training in a paid-drill status should have been recalled to duty before individuals who were not in the active reserve training program. Not only were there claims of inequities in recall procedures, but in many cases reservists who had not been called found it difficult to obtain jobs or to secure promotions because employers were uncertain about how long they could retain employees with reserve obligations.[3] In many cases, improper recalls stemmed from the negligence of the services in keeping up-to-date records on the status of individual reservists.[4] Although most of the difficulties arose in the Army's Organized Reserve Corps, the Navy also provided the basis for numerous complaints.[5]

Long-range military manpower needs were being met by the recruitment of volunteers and the drafting of selected individuals under the Universal Military Training and Service Act.[6] Under the latter system, active duty and reserve service obligations added up to eight years. During the Korean conflict, drafted men who had finished active duty obligations were moving into the reserve components and special provisions had to be made to avoid the recall of these recently-returned veterans. In addition, if the manpower needs for implementing military policy in the cold war were to grind on for years, a stabilized and equitable system of reserve service was needed. It was considered desirable for a greater share of the military manpower needs to be levied on the reserve components than had previously been the case.

A program to establish uniform categories of readiness for all the reserve components of all services and to clarify susceptibility to recall for their members had been under consideration in governmental agencies and in private associations before the outbreak of the Korean hostilities. Much of this effort had taken place in the Department of Defense's Civilian Components Policy Board, first set up by the Secretary of Defense in June, 1949. Although the Board had been reviewing reserve operations since its inception, it stepped up its study in the fall of 1950 by re-examining the whole area of reserve affairs with the intent of formulating policy proposals for legislative action. During this period, the Board held consultations with all military associations and government agencies interested in reserve problems in which they had an opportunity to submit comments on the Board's report to the Secretary of Defense. It was this report that formed the basis for legislative proposals on reserve organization in 1951.[7]

Perhaps the greatest impetus for improvement of the organization and administration of the reserve forces through statute came from members of Congress. Complaints from reservists and their families about the methods of recalling reservists to active duty for the Korean hostilities flooded Congressional offices. There was also a need for a plan to handle men coming out of military service with reserve obligations. Congressmen, in turn, kept prodding the Defense Department for firm legislative proposals to deal with the problems. The call for action was undeniable; Chariman of the House Armed Services Committee Carl Vinson remarked: "We want to know what kind of Reserve we're going to have. It's terrible now." [8]

THE BROOKS SUBCOMMITTEE

Preliminary hearings in the House in the spring of 1951 clarified the place of reserve forces in the American military posture. In testimony before Congressman Overton

Brooks's Special Subcommittee on Reserve Components of the House Armed Services Committee in the spring of 1951 prior to the introduction of a specific bill, Assistant Secretary of Defense Anna Rosenberg indicated the role of the Reserves in national security planning:

> I want to assure members of your committee that we regard the Reserve as an indispensable element in our security. We will not allow it to become a stepchild in the Armed Forces. We are determined to build it stronger and stronger so that we can achieve the high purposes involved in the concept of universal military training and service, and a strong Reserve program. That is the road to a dependable, democratic system of national defense in keeping with the needs and traditions of our country.[9]

Subcommittee member Sterling Cole asked if this view was held also by the professional military people in the Defense Department. Assured by Mrs. Rosenberg that it was, he expressed the hope that the attitude would not change after legislation was enacted.[10]

However, the Defense Department found difficulty in complying with the reserve philosophy expressed by Mrs. Rosenberg. For one thing, it could not be sure of the number of trained men that would be provided until the Universal Military Training and Service Act of 1951 was implemented.[11] Aware of this dilemma, Mrs. Rosenberg, testifying on behalf of a Defense Department Armed Forces Reserve bill, assumed that both the reserve bill and universal military training were part of a joint program. As it turned out, the Universal Military Training and Service Act provided specifically for only a continuation of selective service, although it accepted universal military service in principle. Later the National Guard Association chose to interpret her remarks as meaning that she would withdraw support for the reserve bill if full universal military service was not established. This was one reason for the NGA's change of attitude from active support to mild disagreement with the bill.

The Defense Department's version of the Armed Forces Reserve bill proposed to modernize a mass of long-standing technical legislation. For the purposes of this analysis it is sufficient to focus on only a few of the major sections of the bill designated as H.R. 4860. First, it was to establish seven reserve components for the armed forces, keeping the National Guard separate from the Army and Air Force Reserves. Second, it detailed the conditions for recall to active duty of these component members by establishing three categories—Ready, Standby, and Retired. A ceiling of 1.5 million men was suggested for the Ready Reserve, which could be called to active duty in an emergency declared by the President only in numbers authorized by Congress. Standby and Retired reservists could be called to active duty in Congressionally-declared emergencies.[12]

The appearance of H.R. 4860 in July, 1951, illustrated the speed with which legislative proposals can be prepared when the pressure is unusually great. At the preliminary hearings in April, Mrs. Rosenberg had promised a bill within six months after the House Armed Services Committee indicated the immediate need for a statutory policy on reserve organization and administration. Although such a proposal required the co-ordination of each separate service including the Coast Guard under the Treasury Department and a review by the Bureau of the Budget and the Comptroller, its introduction as H.R. 4860 three months ahead of schedule indicates the high priority attached to its preparation.

INTEREST GROUPS AT WORK

Consideration of the reserve component program in 1951 by the House was extremely thorough. Congressman

Brooks's Special Subcommittee on Reserve Components, comprised of seventeen members, began with an investigation and ended with a specific legislative proposal. A list of those appearing before the subcommittee included all the major interested parties—military associations, veterans' organizations, civilian and military officials.[13] When it was suggested that some of the committee work could have been reduced considerably by closer and more extensive consultation between the Department of Defense and the military associations, Congressman Sterling Cole replied:

> I think if in the future the departments were to adopt that as a policy and accept—not accept, but to receive the counsel and solicit the counsel of the Reserve [Officers] Association representatives and the Guard Association representatives, a great deal of time of Congress will be avoided [*sic*] and these bills could be passed upon with greater degree of unanimity and speed.[14]

Mrs. Rosenberg agreed with this approach as long as her willingness to hear the representatives was not interpreted as acceptance of what was offered.

That reserve organizations should play an important role was recognized not only by Mr. Cole but also by Mr. Brooks. The latter suggested that the National Guard Association and the Reserve Officers Association could file their objections to pending reserve forces legislation with the Special Subcommittee where they would be given a respectful hearing. In addition, they could participate in the executive sessions of the committee when revisions would be considered.

Both organizations took a stand on H.R. 4860. The ROA regarded the bill as a good point of departure for the hearings. Its basic objection to the bill was that the ROA wished to see a maximum amount of the plan written into law, whereas the Pentagon wished to have a minimum included in legislation, thereby leaving a large portion of reserve affairs for administrative resolution. In the later instance, the results could possibly be unfavorable to the ROA.[15]

The attitude of the National Guard Association toward H.R. 4860 is not as easy to characterize. Although the NGA indicated it was well satisfied with existing laws relating to National Guard affairs, it nevertheless did spend considerable time preparing over ninety amendments to the bill covering minor points, most of which were accepted at the markup session on the bill.[16] The revised committee version of the bill, H.R. 5426, did receive a "quite satisfactory" label from the NGA. However, two fears haunted the National Guard; one was the loss of manpower sources and the other was federalization of the Guard. Any references or omissions in the bill that came close to raising these issues received the closest Guard scrutiny. For example, several provisions suggested a greater role for the federal government in supervising reserve administration. In addition, a careful statement of the National Guard role had not been stated in the bill.

After extensive study and revision in committee, the Armed Forces Reserve bill as H.R. 5426 encountered little opposition on the House floor and passed by voice vote on October 15, 1951. Congressman Arthur Winstead illustrated the time and careful effort spent by the Subcommittee on Reserve Components:

> I sat in daily attendance with representatives of every prominent Reserve and veterans' organization while the bill was studied, written, and rewritten, paragraph by paragraph and line by line. The subcommittee did not pass from one portion of the bill to another until we had substantial agreement between those gathered around the table.[17]

Another member of the full committee on Armed Services, Congressman Dewey Short, commented on the significance of the agreement on a reserve bill for the first time between all groups—the National Defense Establishment, the reserve components and their representative associations, and the veterans' organizations.[18] All signs pointed to smooth sailing in the Senate.

UNIVERSAL MILITARY TRAINING IS DEFEATED

Before the Senate acted on this proposal for a revised reserve program as set forth in H.R. 5426, the House turned down a related bill to put universal military training into operation in March, 1952. Although only the principle of universal military training had been approved in the Universal Military Training and Service Act of 1951, the hope of the Defense Department sponsors had been that universal military training would be fully implemented by Congress and become a full-fledged companion to the Armed Forces Reserve Act. The plan embodied in H.R. 5904 proposing universal military service would have provided an abundant supply of young recruits for the reserve components. The Reserve Officers Association showed its concern that it might lose out completely if the reserve bill failed to pass by stating in its monthly magazine: "With the temporary shelving of UMT, individuals indisposed to the 'Magna Carta' for reservists began passing the word that the Reserve bill was incapable of operating without UMT."[19] It went on to make a plea for favorable action on the Reserve bill to prevent complete erosion of the reserve forces. At least the planners of the Department of Defense now knew what manpower resources they had to work with in a reserve program as it came before the Senate for action.

The failure to secure passage of universal military training as embodied in the National Security Training Corps bill (H.R. 5904) triggered the withdrawal of the National Guard Association's support of the Armed Forces Reserve bill. Although the NGA offered fears of federalization of the

Guard and placing too great a burden on veterans of the reserve forces as reasons for its action, the most important reason centered on National Guard manpower procurement problems.[20] Establishment of universal military training would have presented a solution to their problem. The NGA supported the reserve forces bill as long as it helped the cause of universal military training. When the latter failed, the National Guard admitted that the reserve bill would do nothing to help it maintain its authorized strength.[21]

Although the National Guard Association's change of mind on H.R. 5426 was significant and might have spoiled the day, all other interested parties stayed firmly behind the bill. Mrs. Rosenberg pointed out that the NGA was objecting to amendments which the Guard itself had sponsored and which had been accepted in the House bill. Military associations and veterans' groups reasserted their support.[22] The NGA and the ROA fired verbal salvos at each other, questioning whether they really represented their respective membership and associated personnel.[23]

Without universal military training, H.R. 5426 still contained features of benefit to the National Guard. Among these features were those that dealt with allowances, transfer, and promotion. By withdrawing support for the bill, the National Guard could enjoy the benefits of the bill without using any of its "credit," which might be expended in the passage of other legislative proposals. It could not be put in the position of having received something for which it had asked. If the Reserve bill failed and the NGA had worked for its passage, then it would still have been without universal military training, and it would have lost part of its reputation for effectiveness.[24]

Few changes were made in H.R. 5426 on its way to final approval. Loss of National Guard support did not at the same time mean active Guard opposition. The Senate lessened the susceptibility of veterans to recall, but this action was overturned in the conference committee, which upheld the division of personnel available for active duty call into Ready and Standby categories. The Ready Reserve of 1.5 million men, which included the entire National Guard, could be called to active duty in an emergency declared by the President. Those in the Standby Reserve could be called to active duty only by Congressional authority. Final passage came on July 9, 1952.[25]

PARTICIPANTS REMAIN DIVIDED

Comment on the Armed Forces Reserve Act of 1952 was divided between the optimistic, which included the Defense Department and the Reserve Officers Association, and the pessimistic, comprised of the National Guard and prominent military analysts. The Department of Defense, which had pushed hard for passage, still saw the need for universal military training but felt that the burden of national service was equalized within the reserve forces.[26] The Reserve Officers Association considered the Act as the accomplishment of a priority mission, since it incorporated into law hundreds of needed features for the personnel of the reserve forces.[27] However, the ROA was still busily working out the detailed regulations required to execute the Act with each of the services at their invitation during the remainder of 1952. Its mode of operation was "to support the services when justified . . . convert them to ROA beliefs when occasion demanded . . . object strenuously to any move that would prove detrimental."[28]

National Guard Association commentary was somewhat ambivalent. The Act incorporated many safeguards insisted upon by the NGA, including the retention of the National Guard Bureau in its current status. At the same time the NGA felt the program would not work as a total system.

Guard spokesmen denied that the Act was a "Magna Carta" for reserve forces.[29] In the last sentiment the Guard was joined by two of its usually strongest critics, generally considered outstanding military commentators. Walter Millis found the Act still a long way from a "Magna Carta" for reservists and announced:

> The truth is that the new Reserve Act neither provides for an effectively mobilizable reserve nor relieves the drafted man from the obligations now imposed on him. It is largely a sham system. And so our reserve system will certainly remain until Congress has the courage really to face up to the problem of the military obligation in a democratic society.[30]

Hanson Baldwin saw the Act as only a first step in the problem of creating adequate reserve forces. He felt that any effort for the reserve program that took priority away from regular forces might even be a step backward.[31] Both writers disparaged the preservation of the concept that civilian soldiers could occupy the first line of defense in an era of great military technological changes.

EXPERIENCE UNDER THE 1952 ACT

Early reports of difficulty in securing the voluntary participation of returning servicemen in the reserve programs became a familiar story during the first few years of the Eisenhower administration.[32] It was hoped that men with a statutory obligation in the Ready Reserve would participate in voluntary training in order to establish eligibility for early transfer to the less vulnerable Standby Reserve. This was not the case for the Army. Instead the Ready Reserve created by the Reserve Act of 1952 tended to develop into a pool of manpower available for call to active duty rather than groups of well-organized and well-trained reservists participating in drills and summer field training.

A subcommittee of the Senate Armed Services Committee confirmed these difficulties and declared the shortage of enlisted personnel to be the primary problem confronting the reserve forces. The subcommittee claimed that the Armed Forces Reserve Act of 1952 was not accomplishing its intended objective—namely, stimulating former servicemen to participate in active reserve units. Manpower shortages were found in the Ready Reserve categories of all civilian components, with those in the Army Reserve being especially crucial.[33] Recommendations of this Senate subcommittee pointed to the need for legislation that would supply the means by which an active program could be made more attractive to the young men of the nation. It was also suggested that some compulsory reserve training program might be essential.

Studies by two agencies of the executive branch formed the basis for administration proposals that eventually were embodied in the National Reserve Plan and introduced in 1955 as the Reserve Forces Act of that year. One was conducted by the National Security Training Commission, which had been created under the Universal Military Training and Service Act of 1951 and had been unable to gain acceptance for universal military training in 1952. In its report in December, 1953, the Commission suggested a system of national security training of six months to be followed by service in a reserve component for seven and one-half years as a solution to what it regarded as an unsatisfactory reserve system.[34]

The Office of Defense Mobilization had also been requested by the President to make a study of military manpower problems and to recommend any needed changes. Its report proposed an "immediately callable Reserve" and a "selectively callable Reserve" to meet the national security requirements as determined by the National Security Council and the Department of Defense.[35] Acting on these recommendations, President Eisenhower then asked the heads of both agencies to draft a plan for a revised reserve system. Reserve mobilization requirements developed by the Department of Defense were then incorporated into the plan by the Office of Defense Mobilization before it was presented to the National Security Council on June 17, 1954. This National Reserve Plan was finally approved by the National Security Council in November, 1954, after it had been further revised by the Defense Department and the Office of Defense Mobilization.[36] President Eisenhower then used this plan as the basis for his legislative recommendations on reserve forces policy to Congress in 1955.

THE NATIONAL RESERVE PLAN

Besides the difficulties encountered in working out an effective reserve program, the impending expiration of the Selective Service Act on July 1, 1955, added impetus to an administration desire to seek legislative manpower decisions in that year.[37] In his message to Congress on January 13, 1955, President Eisenhower combined recommendations for a four-year extension of the draft with a plan to strengthen the reserve forces.[38] The National Reserve Plan came to be described as the "New Look." As outlined by the President, it was designed to provide the type of forces necessary to meet successfully the challenges to United States security and to world peace without invoking burdens that would endanger the liberties or the economic system the nation was determined to defend. Embodied in the "New Look" were two ideas: (1) although the policy of containment would be continued, large ground armies were no longer justified with the existence of nuclear weapons; and (2) any cut in active ground forces could be compensated for, in part at least, by an improved state of readiness in the reserve forces.

Thus, the National Reserve Plan in the form of H.R. 2967 was launched with full presidential backing. Essentially the bill contained three modifications to existing reserve force legislative provisions. First, the Ready Reserve would stress the training of individuals and units so that their state of military readiness would make them available for recall during the early part of a general mobilization. This group would be increased from 1.5 million men to 2.9 million men, and the President would be authorized to order up to one million reservists to duty in a national emergency proclaimed by him. For those who chose to serve under the plan, satisfactory participation in reserve activities would be rewarded by a reduction of time spent in the Ready Reserve, whereas refusal to participate in training with reserve units would be penalized by the imposition of additional periods of extended active duty. Second, to secure a supply of young reservists with basic training completed, a program of controlled quotas would provide an opportunity for those who had not yet reached the age of nineteen to take six months of active duty and to fulfil the remainder of their obligation with service in the reserves. Third, in relation to the National Guard, all recruits would be required to complete six months of active-duty basic training. If Guard membership rolls fell below the authorized levels, then transfer to the Guard of desirable quantities of men returning from active duty would be permitted. Special state defense forces in addition to the Guard would be authorized in time of peace.[39]

Legislative action on the National Reserve Plan exhibited distinctive characteristics of a recognizable pattern in reserve forces policy-making. In the attempt to establish statutory manpower policy for the reserve components of all military services, Congress became involved in a maze of complex technical aspects, which even the most dedicated subcommittee member found difficult to follow. This resulted partly from the demands of interest groups for assurances that detailed policy be placed in the statutes and partly from the desire of Congress to assert its will in executive fields. In this process a large share of the extensive deliberations was left to senior congressmen, executive specialists, and experienced representatives of military associations, such as the National Guard Association and the Reserve Officers Association. The individual capabilities of these participants and the support they could muster became extremely important elements in the creation of the final legislative product.

The Eisenhower administration wanted its Reserve Plan adopted and wanted it badly. One House Armed Services Committee member remarked, "If you have any imagination you can realize some of the pressures that have been brought on me from the Pentagon and I was also called to the White House."[40] The President of the National Guard Association claimed that the pressure from the Defense Department was continuous, utterly ruthless—not equaled in his thirty years of legislative experience.[41] Soon after Strom Thurmond reached the Senate on a surprising write-in victory in 1954, he was greeted in a private meeting by President Eisenhower and asked for the support of the Reserve Officers Association, which he was then serving as its president. Space for two major articles by Carter Burgess, Assistant Secretary of Defense for Manpower and Reserves, was made available in the monthly magazine of the ROA.[42] In one appearance before the House Armed Services Subcommittee No. 1 on H.R. 2967, Senator Thurmond said that the ROA amendments on minor points in the bill would make improvements but that the administration version should pass even if his amendments were not accepted.[43] In the area of legislative policy-making for the armed forces reserve, the strong backing of the Defense Department aided by a major military association supplied considerable momentum for a bill.

Despite this pressure, however, the objections of a major interested party can be the cause for substantial revision of the bill. The National Guard Association had major criticisms of the administration bill (H.R. 2967), which centered largely on its failure to assure sufficient personnel for National Guard needs and goals.[44] A substitute version written by the House Armed Services Committee (H.R. 5297) overcame these difficulties but, in turn, was blocked by an amendment from Congressman Adam Clayton Powell. In this case the Powell amendment was aimed at prohibiting the transfer of those with reserve obligations to National Guard units in states where segregation was practiced.[45] To overcome this combination of objections, Chairman Carl Vinson of the Armed Services Committee in the House introduced H.R. 7000, which omitted almost all provisions dealing with the National Guard. In this form the bill passed the House without difficulty. The transformation was described by one military writer as a situation in which the "compulsory military reserve bill became the subject of intensive artificial respiration."[46] Any concern over National Guard Association opposition was dispelled by its president when he indicated that the Guard did not desire to be included in the bill, that he was satisfied with existing laws, and that he hoped the bill would prove beneficial for other reserve components.[47] The final steps involved relatively minor hurdles, and the bill became law on August 9, 1955.[48]

In signing the bill, President Eisenhower stated that the reserve structure would be strengthened in the following ways:

1. It provides a statutory means of assuring that our Federal Reserves will be composed of prior-trained men on a planned basis.

2. It will permit an increase in the Ready Reserve manpower ceiling from 1,500,000 to 2,900,000.

3. It clearly establishes the obligation to participate in Reserve training and provides for effective and reasonable enforcement measures to achieve this participation.

4. It authorizes the President to order up one million Ready Reservists in an emergency proclaimed by him.[49]

At the same time the President put the National Guard on notice that he was not satisfied with its withdrawal from the bill because it left serious doubts in his mind that the National Guard could attain its planned size and the necessary standards of military proficiency and readiness. A continuing review of National Guard programs and standards was to be conducted by the Secretary of Defense and the Joint Chiefs of Staff.

EVALUATION

Provisions of the Reserve Acts of 1952 and 1955 brought greater uniformity to the structure of the reserve forces and the hope for a program that would manifest greater readiness and effectiveness.[50] The use of manpower in the reserve components was clarified. The armed services came as close as possible to getting the benefits of universal military training without actually having such a program established. Since the National Guard was not significantly changed, most of the features of the laws represented a catching up, primarily by the Army Reserve, with the National Guard's early postwar start in growth. As a result of its legislative efforts, Congress was hoping that the professional military personnel would now give more attention to careful implementation of the laws relating to the reserve components.

The manpower decisions represented in these two measures were consistent with the strategic objective of containment of Communist forces or any major effort to disturb world peace. The "New Look" in military manpower policy was predicated on a large mobilization base of reserve forces to meet any all-out emergency. This fostered the persistent criticism that any support for reserve forces at the expense of the regulars would be a poor decision. There was fear that emphasis placed on the reserve concept by these laws would detract from military professionalism.[51]

When a comparison is made of the legislative decision-making process involved in these two Reserve Acts with that involved in the reserve retirement law of 1948, significant differences do appear. In 1952 and 1955 a consolidated Defense Department made a co-ordinated effort to secure a legislative policy decision after listening to recommendations from interest groups. It was now clear to military associations that invitation to consultation from the Department of Defense did not mean any administration predisposition to accept the association proposals. The National Guard Association and the Reserve Officers Association were not working together on these two laws as they had on the reserve retirement law. Each continued to show the same competence by Congressional standards in dealing with complex technical aspects of military manpower problems, but each used some of its energies to counteract the influence and reputation of the other. The National Guard Association was outflanked by the Reserve Officers Association on both reserve bills; the NGA was most effective in a negative way by preventing features unwanted by the National Guard from being enacted into law.

Congress remained sympathetic and non-partisan in its approach to the military reserve program, but it did become temporarily divided on a sectional basis on the point of transferring reservists into National Guard units in which segregation was practiced. Armed Services Committees, especially in the House, were willing to expend unusual amounts of time and energy on the most detailed items in order to accommodate interest groups. In 1955 the Democratic Congress had no more trouble working with the Republican President in the area of reserve forces policy-making than a Republican Congress did with the Democratic President in 1948. Within the two houses, the final bill received overwhelming support after the issue of segregation had temporarily inflamed sectional feeling.

Compared with the reserve retirement law of 1948, the two reserve acts just considered seemed to bring forth a better rapport between regular and reserve personnel. At the same time there were still issues that brought each group into sharp disagreement. Such was the case when promotion criteria and procedures for reserve officers came under consideration during the deliberations prior to the passage of the Reserve Officer Personnel Act of 1954, or ROPA, as it is better known to members of the reserve forces. An analysis of legislative action on this Act should provide another valuable measure of the policy-making process for armed forces reserve components. This will be found in the next chapter.

Footnotes

1. House Committee on Armed Services, *Armed Forces Reserve Act of 1951*, H. Rept. 1066 to accompany H.R. 5426, 82d Cong., 1st sess., 1951, pp. 5–11. The multitude of laws creating the different service reserves starts with the Dick Act of 1903.

2. 66 *Stat.* 481 (1952) and 69 *Stat.* 598 (1955).

3. House Committee on Armed Services, *Hearings, Reserve Components*, H.R. 4860, 82d Cong., 1st sess., 1951, pp. 6–7.

4. *Congressional Record*, 82d Cong., 1st sess., 1951, p. 13160.

5. Henry G. Doyle, "Speaking Frankly—Part II," *Reserve Officer*, XXVIII (April, 1951), 12–14.

6. 66 *Stat.* 604 (1948) as amended by 65 *Stat.* 75 (1951). The first is referred to as the Selective Service Act of 1948 and the second as the Universal Military Training and Service Act of 1951.

7. House Committee on Armed Services, *Hearings, Reserve Components*, H.R. 4860, 82d Cong., 1st sess., 1951, pp. 191, 219, 371. Edwin H. Burgess, Chairman of the Civilian Components Policy Board from May, 1950, to June, 1951, left the position shortly after the Board was renamed the Reserve Forces Policy Board.

8. "Washington Newsletter," *Reserve Officer*, XXVIII (March, 1951), 1.

9. House Committee on Armed Services, *Hearings, Reserve Components*, H.R. 4860, 82d Cong., 1st sess., 1951, p. 190.

10. *Ibid.*, p. 194.

11. 65 *Stat.* 75 (1951).

12. House Committee on Armed Services, *Hearings, Reserve Components*, H.R. 4860, 82d Cong., 1st sess., 1951, pp. 305–20. See chap. i, note 2 *supra*.

13. *Ibid.*, pp. iii-iv.

14. *Ibid.*, p. 519.

15. *Reserve Officer*, XXVIII (November, 1951), 2.

16. *Official Proceedings of the National Guard Association of the United States*, 73d General Conference, October 22–24, 1951, p. 246.

17. *Congressional Record*, 82d Cong., 1st sess., 1951, p. 13160.

18. *Ibid.*, p. 19158.

19. "ROA Washington Newsletter," *Reserve Officer*, XXVIII (April, 1952), 1.

20. "Washington Report," *National Guardsman*, VI (April, 1952), 12.

21. Senate Committee on Armed Services, *Hearings, Armed Forces Reserve Act of 1952*, H.R. 5426, 82d Cong., 2d sess., 1952, pp. 108, 110, 119.

22. *Ibid.*, pp. 174, 178, 194, 248. These included the ROA, the Marine Corps Reserve Officers Association, the Air Reserve Association, and the Military Order of the World Wars.

23. "ROA Washington Newsletter," *Reserve Officer*, XXVIII (July, 1952), 1; and "The President's Page," *National Guardsman*, VI (August, 1952), 4.

24. "Washington Report," *National Guardsman*, VI (April, 1952), 12.

25. 66 *Stat.* 481 (1952).

26. Department of Defense, *Semiannual Report of the Secretary of Defense, January 1–June 30, 1952*, pp. 15–16.

27. "ROA Washington Newsletter," *Reserve Officer*, XXVIII (August, 1952), 1.

28. *Ibid.*, XXVIII (October, 1952), 1.

29. *Official Proceedings of the National Guard Association of the United States*, 74th General Conference, October 6–9, 1952, p. 268.

30. Walter Millis, "The Reserves," *New York Herald-Tribune*, December 7, 1952, Section 2, p. 4.

31. Hanson Baldwin, "Faults in the Reserve Act," *New York Times*, July 15, 1952, p. 15.

32. Department of Defense, *Semiannual Report of the Secretary of Defense, January 1–June 30, 1953*, p. 25. Also see the *Semiannual Report* for the period January 1–June 30, 1955, p. 19.

33. Senate Committee on Armed Services, Interim Subcommittee on Preparedness, *Status of Reserve and National Guard Forces of the Armed Services*, Second Report, 83d Cong., 2d sess., 1954, p. iii.

34. National Security Training Commission, *20th Century Minutemen*, A Report to the President (Washington, D.C.: Government Printing Office, December 1, 1953), pp. 123–28.

35. Office of Defense Mobilization, *Manpower Resources for National Security*, A Report to the President by the Director (Washington, D.C.: Government Printing Office, January 6, 1954), pp. iii–v.

36. House Committee on Armed Services, *National Reserve Plan*, H. Rept. 457 to accompany H.R. 5297, 84th Cong., 1st sess., 1955, p. 3.

37. Mr. Bryce N. Harlow, former Chief Clerk of the House Armed Services Committee following World War II and later Special Assistant to President Eisenhower, indicated that major decisions on reserve policy matters are usually made only when crisis-type situations arise. Until then they remain "simmering on the back burner." Interview conducted in Washington, D.C., on May 27, 1964.

38. House, *Military Security of the United States*, Doc. No. 68, Message from the President of the United States, 84th Cong., 1st sess., 1955, pp. 2–4.

39. House Committee on Armed Services, *Hearings, National Reserve Plan*, H.R. 2967, Committee Paper No. 11, 84th Cong., 1st sess., 1955, pp. 1244–50.

40. *Congressional Record*, 84th Cong., 1st sess., 1955, p. 9789.

41. *Official Proceedings of the National Guard Association of the United States*, 77th General Conference, October 17–20, 1955, p. 228.

42. *Reserve Officer*, XXXI (January, 1955), 1; and XXXI (March, 1955), 9.

43. House Committee on Armed Services, *Hearings, National Reserve Plan*, H.R. 2967, Committee Paper No. 11, 84th Cong., 1st sess., 1955, p. 1771.

44. *Ibid.*, p. 2223.

45. *Congressional Record*, 84th Cong., 1st sess., 1955, pp. 6487, 6541, 6645.

46. Hanson Baldwin, "Objections to the Reserve Bill," *New York Times*, June 9, 1955, p. 16.

47. Senate Committee on Armed Services, *Hearings, National Reserve Plan*, H.R. 2967, Committee Paper No. 11, 84th Cong., 1st sess., 1955, p. 28.

48. Earlier, on June 30, 1955, the related legislation on the draft extended the Selective Service Act for four years (69 *Stat.* 223 [1955]).

49. *New York Times*, August 10, 1955, p. 10.

50. Further uniformity was achieved under 77 *Stat.* 134 (1963), in which a six-year military obligation was established for all those entering the military services for the first time whether by induction, enlistment in the regular or reserve forces, or graduation from an ROTC program. The number of years an individual spends on active duty and the number of years he spends in a reserve component vary with the service and the program through which one enters, but the total will equal six, with few exceptions.

51. Hanson Baldwin, "Objections to the Reserve Bill," *New York Times*, June 9, 1955, p. 16.

4

PROMOTION AND PRECEDENCE
Reserve Officer Personnel Act of 1954

4

PROMOTION AND PRECEDENCE
Reserve Officer Personnel Act of 1954

ORIGINALLY it was intended that the Armed Forces Reserve Act of 1952 should include such personnel provisions for reserve officers as promotion, precedence, grade structure, retention, and elimination. These hopes were shelved temporarily because the problems were too complex to handle at the time. Instead it was decided to make a separate study of these personnel matters.[1] Guidance for such study was given in a section of the 1952 Act directing each service Secretary to establish an equitable promotion system for officers of the reserve components in an active status either on duty with the active forces or in the reserve program. The goal of Congress was to have in statutory form a promotion system that would parallel as closely as practicable the one followed for regular officers and be as uniform as possible among all services.[2] Although its system was not in statute, the Navy procedure tended to serve as a model for other military departments to follow in developing a system to meet their specific requirements.

As the Korean conflict drew to a close, it became apparent that a peacetime military establishment would involve a higher level of activity for both regular and reserve forces than had ever been the case in American history. Pressure for a more permanent system of promotion and precedence in the reserve components began to build as the prospects for more interaction between regular and reserve officers on active duty became more likely and as the long-term involvement of reservists in an active training program became a reality. Within an over-all atmosphere of continued American containment of the Communist world, the details of a personnel policy for reserve officers was handled in the manner of domestic politics.

Full consideration was given to a statutory promotion and precedence system for reserve officers by the Eighty-third Congress. The product became known as the Reserve Officer Personnel Act of 1954 (ROPA). In this chapter attention is focused on the principle of allowing credit for satisfactory inactive duty reserve participation in the process of determining promotion service and precedence (date of rank). This approach was adopted because this principle is the major underlying feature of an extremely complicated act. No attempt will be made to present all the substantive details of each service's reserve officer promotion system that finally emerged in law. An analysis of the way this principle was woven into procedures for promotion of reserve officers will provide another illustration of how policy for the reserve components has developed through the legisaltive process. It presents an opportunity to view a Republican President and Congress offering leadership in the search for solutions to rather complex personnel problems of the armed forces.

PRESSURE FOR RESERVE PROMOTION PLAN

A variety of factors created pressure for the establishment of a reserve promotion system that would parallel the system for regular officers set forth in the Officer Personnel Act of 1947.[3] Experience from the recall of reserve officers for the Korean conflict emphasized some of the inconsistencies in the treatment of regular and reserve officers. After completing two years of duty in the Korean hostilities, many veteran reserve officers found themselves still in the same grade in which they had finished World War II. At the same time accelerated promotions for regular officers widened the gap between regular and reserve officer promotion procedures. In the Air Force Reserve, officers were serving on active duty below their permanent grade while regular officers were being promoted above their permanent grade.[4]

There were several other factors also generating pressure for the establishment of a reserve officer promotion system patterned after the procedure used for regulars. Congress continued to support the military philosophy of a small standing army backed by ready, well-trained reserves. Since the citizen-soldiers of the reserve components comprised the vast majority of those who had to bear arms during times of war or national emergency, Congress accepted the approach that it should encourage active participation in the reserve program and that a firm promotion policy was necessary to furnish the incentive for that participation.[5]

Members of the federal reserve components were also eager to see reserve officers attain positions in the top command structure. The National Guard was quite sensitive about the removal of some of its top commanders from large units during World War II. A statutory promotion system patterned after the procedure for regular officers would supposedly permit reservists to reach positions well up in the hierarchy of command. Major General Ellard Walsh, President of the National Guard Association, was not particularly hopeful that ROPA would be very helpful in this regard since the Navy and Marine Corps Reserves, already using a type of plan proposed in ROPA, had fared very poorly in their number of general and flag officers compared with the Guard's total of approximately two hundred general officers.[6] Senator Margaret Chase Smith, a strong supporter of the reservists, believed that the only reason the regulars were fighting the attempt to establish a statutory promotion system for reserve officers was that they simply did not want officers with high rank in the reserves, because they would be a threat to the ability of regulars to accelerate their temporary promotions at a time of full mobilization.[7]

Another factor that increased efforts to press for action on a reserve promotion bill was the feeling of reserve officers that promotion procedures should be spelled out specifically in statute. Colonel Charles M. Boyer, Executive Director of the Reserve Officers Association, and Major General Melvin Maas, Chairman of its Legislative Committee, urged Representative Leroy Johnson, subcommittee chairman, to prevail upon Dewey Short, Chairman of the House Armed Services Committee, to advise the Secretary of Defense that hearings on the reserve promotion bill should be scheduled not later than May 27. Mr. Short agreed, and the hearings did actually start on that date.[8]

The basis for the House hearings was H.R. 1222, which had been introduced on January 7, 1953, by Congressman Overton Brooks.[9] At the heart of the bill was the concept of periodic, mandatory consideration and selection of commissioned officers of the reserve components for promotion. Upon completion of stated periods of service in various grades, officers would be considered for promotion without regard to the availability of positions in organized units to accommodate those promoted. Although reservists could be sure of consideration for promotion at least within a specified period of time, there were two unwelcome aspects in this proposed system. First, if a reservist received a promotion, he could, in effect, be promoted out of an organized unit and consequently out of drill-pay status if there were no position in the unit to accommodate the higher grade. At the same time units would lose experienced personnel because the unit organizational structure restricted positions to certain grades. The reservist could still remain active, however, in a unit that could accommodate his grade or as an individual in a pool. Second, failure to be selected for promotion on two occasions could mean removal from an active reserve status.

In addition to the promotion and retention procedures, several other features were among the provisions of H.R. 1222. Total authorized reserve officer strengths as well as the distribution within grades were to be determined by the Secretary of each service.[10] The desired result of the system was a steady flow of promotion for reserve officers and the elimination of unqualified officers just as the Officer Personnel Act of 1947 had worked for regular officers.

H.R. 1222 had been drafted by the Department of Defense with reluctance. The Reserve Act of 1952 had directed the Secretary of each service to establish an equitable promotion system for reserve officers, and the House Armed Services Committee insisted that the Defense Department submit a legislative proposal for this purpose in 1953. In compliance with the 1952 Act, the services had already brought in a new promotion system under administrative regulations. Regular officers of the Army and the Air Force in the Pentagon were opposed to putting these regulations into statute and placing reserve officers on an equal promotional footing by allowing constructive credit for inactive training time in computing date of rank, or precedence. The regulars were neither eager to have the additional competition for active duty promotions from reserve officers, which is a separate matter, nor pleased at the prospect of reservists moving up through the higher grades in reserve training and then being mobilized at those grades in emergencies. At the same time a new administration was about to assume responsibility for executive decisions, and it had indicated a desire to study the reserve area thoroughly before submitting any detailed legislative recommendations. H.R. 1222 had been submitted as a result of constant Congressional prodding; the Defense Department was therefore hesitant about testifying on it at an early date.

PATTERN OF CONFLICT IN THE HOUSE

House action on H.R. 1222 began with extensive hearings and culminated in the passage of a substitute bill during the closing minutes of the first session of the Eighty-third Congress. Representative Leroy Johnson chaired the Reserve Subcommittee for the hearings as he had done for the reserve retirement bill in 1948. It was a subcommittee sympathetic with the reserve position, which was represented very strongly by the Reserve Officers Association. In the intricate give and take of subcommittee sessions, respect seemed to grow for those with experience and expertise among the committee members, the professional staff, and the military association representatives.

The pattern of conflict for the hearings was one that pitted Army and Air Force officers from the Defense Department against the Reserve Officers Association. The subcommittee tended to sustain the ROA position while the National Guard Association agreed with the Army and Air Force initially before finally changing its mind and giving assent to a substitute bill. Although the Department of Defense had not been enthusiastic about translating any reserve promotion system into statute, the major provisions of the plan as proposed in H.R. 1222 were finally supported by Army and Air Force officers representing the Defense Department.

Three changes in H.R. 1222 were advocated by the representatives of the Reserve Officers Association.[11] First, they proposed in the matter of precedence for all services that the date of rank and the date of commission be the same, a situation that already existed in the Navy. Time would accrue toward promotional eligibility from the date of commission if it were spent either on active duty or in satisfactory reserve participation. Second, the ROA requested statutory provision for a quota of reserve officers for each of the military services.[12] Third, it was felt that within each reserve component there should be a specific number of officers in each grade specified by law. In neither of the latter two situations did the ROA feel that the decision should be left to the Secretary of each service.

Outside of the committee members themselves, the most active participant in the hearings was Colonel Charles M. Boyer, the Executive Director of the Reserve Officers Association. With a background of active duty in the Pentagon in reserve personnel affairs during the latter part of World War II and with an apprenticeship on the ROA staff under its former executive director, Brigadier General E. A. Evans, Colonel Boyer had detailed knowledge of reserve personnel matters that was often tapped in the hearings.

Colonel Boyer was assisted by Major General Melvin Maas who had perhaps the ideal qualifications for establishing credibility before this House Armed Services subcommittee. He had been in Congress for sixteen years; he had a fine war record as a Marine Corps Reserve general; and he was at that time Chairman of the Legislative Committee of the ROA, Chairman of the Board of the Marine Corps Reserve Officers Association, and Commander-in-Chief of the Military Order of the World Wars. In 1938 General Maas had participated as a congressman in the development of a statutory promotion system for the Navy (called the running mate system), which gave reserve officers promotional equality with regular Navy officers and which would still be retained in H.R. 1222.

General Maas's vigorous support of the ROA position received a most favorable reception from subcommittee members. He claimed that the Navy objected to the running mate system prior to its adoption just as the Army and Air Force were objecting to the promotion bill in 1953, but that now the Navy was happy with its system. He also contended that the regulars of the Army did not want reserve officers in senior ranks eligible to take command of large units during a mobilization.[13]

The defense of the Army and the Air Force position for the Pentagon was carried primarily by two field grade reserve officers who had remained on active duty for a career. Their case rested on a series of four arguments that Congress found hard to accept. First, new regulations for promotion had been in operation only a short time and deserved a longer period of trial before putting them into statutory form; second, the military experience and proficiency levels necessary for promotion either on active duty or in the reserve program could be attained best through active duty performance of military duties; third, any fixed total number or grade distribution within a com-

ponent established without a specific basis for application
was unrealistic; and fourth, such determination should be
left to the Secretary of each respective service.[14] Although
the two reserve officers from the Pentagon were exception-
ally competent and their espousal of a position in opposition
to the ROA could have been expected to weaken the ROA's
stand, the fact that regular officers of the general officer
level did not lead off the presentation reduced what otherwise might have been a very effective impact. Civilian leaders at the Pentagon also chose to refrain from appearing at
the House hearings.[15]

The National Guard Association initially opposed several
sections of H.R. 1222 in the House hearings but finally
accepted the substitute bill, which made important changes
in the original bill. Although the NGA usually preferred
statutory provisions over administrative regulations in the
establishment of personnel policy, in this case it agreed with
the Army and Air Force viewpoint that a longer trial period
should be used to test the regulations formulated after the
Reserve Act of 1952 was put into effect. President of NGA,
Major General Ellard Walsh, could point to an enviable
picture of promotion opportunity in the National Guard
when comparing it with the Navy and Marine Corps Reserves, which had already been giving credit for promotion
eligibility to reservists as the ROA was requesting. In the
Air National Guard there was the possibility that promotion
to a higher grade would mean a loss of some experienced
personnel because units would lack sufficient positions to
accommodate higher grades in increased quantity. However,
when the NGA examined the revised bill, H.R. 6573, it saw
no reason to oppose it. The modifications did not significantly affect the National Guard officer promotion system.[16]

The revised bill that emerged from the hearings incorporated the major suggestions of the Reserve Officers Association but still retained about 90 per cent of the Defense

Department's recommendations. The date of commission was accepted as the date of rank for the determination of eligibility for consideration in reserve promotion procedures as long as service in that grade was satisfactory. Reserve officer strength allotments for each civilian component and grade distribution within each component were placed in the bill rather than left to the decision of each service Secretary.[17]

Passage of the revised bill by the House was facilitated by committee thoroughness and interest group action. The importance of subcommittee work can be judged by some of the remarks of the congressmen not on the Armed Services Committee. They admitted that they did not have the time to make a detailed analysis of the bill but that they could vote for it with confidence because they had complete trust and faith in the work of the subcommittee members. Besides the intensive effort spent on the complex aspects of writing and rewriting each paragraph of the bill with subcommittee members and representatives of the National Guard Association at the national level, the Reserve Officers Association also aroused its membership to urge House members to seek a vote on the measure before the adjournment deadline. With just a few hours to go in the session before adjournment, the Reserve Officer Personnel bill passed the House unanimously.[18]

SCENE OF ACTION SHIFTS TO THE SENATE

In the second session of the Eighty-third Congress, the scene of action for ROPA shifted to the Senate. Proponents of the bill had the tasks of first securing hearings and then resisting amendments to H.R. 6573; this was the goal of the Reserve Officers Association and the hope of Senator

Margaret Chase Smith, perhaps the strongest senatorial supporter of the reserves. As the Senate was being urged to have hearings by the ROA, the Defense Department was in the process of formulating a new plan for the reserve program based on the findings from studies by the National Security Training Commission and the Office of Defense Mobilization referred to in the last chapter.[19] The top specialist for Reserve and Manpower, Assistant Secretary of Defense John A. Hannah, requested that the hearings be delayed until that plan took legislative form.[20] The first day's hearings on April 22, 1954, were held to fulfil an obligation to reserve force organizations as explained by Senator Leverett Saltonstall, Chairman of the Armed Services Committee, but he tended to agree with Dr. Hannah's suggestion for delay when he observed that a great deal of staff work remained to be done on the complex provisions of ROPA.[21]

The second and final day of hearings came almost three months later on July 20 with little change in participant attitudes. For their defense of H.R. 6573 the ROA had a team of four experienced protagonists.[22] Their defense of the bill reviewed the need for improving reserve officer morale, the need to stimulate participation in the reserve program, the need for senior reserve officers, and the value of the reserve components in time of war.

Delay or modification of H.R. 6573 was the goal that guided the presentations of the Department of Defense and the separate service departments in the second day of Senate hearings, which had been somewhat reluctantly resumed by Senator Saltonstall at the urging of Major General Maas.[23] Inasmuch as Dr. Hannah could not provide evidence of the nature of any new plan for the reserve program, the representatives from the Pentagon had to proceed with an examination of the bill already under consideration and to concentrate on the modification of the most objectionable sections—those which, in this case, the Reserve Officers Association was firmly pledged to preserve. On the matter of time in grade for precedence and promotion, Dr. Hannah doubted the effectiveness of the Navy system already existing, which credited Naval and Marine Corps Reserve officers with all calendar time in grade for the purposes of determining eligibility for promotion whether the time was on active or inactive duty. Thomas S. Gates, Undersecretary of the Navy, pointed out that the Navy was considering a revision of its running mate system because it was too inflexible and because complete consistency of any revised promotion system with the whole new reserve program would be more certain if all pending legislative proposals would be considered together. Hugh Milton, Assistant Secretary of the Army for Manpower and Reserve Forces, bore down on the manner in which the establishment of specific numbers and percentages of those numbers in each grade of the Army Reserve would create serious obstacles for the Secretary of the Army in endeavoring to constitute a reserve officers corps of numbers in grades necessary to meet mobilization requirements.[24]

Both the National Guard Association and the Air Force Association agreed with the Pentagon presentations. General Walsh, as he had done previously in the House hearings, indicated that H.R. 6573 did nothing for the Army and Air National Guard and that the conditions had changed enough in the development of a new reserve program that the Department of Defense should be given an opportunity to submit the new plan for the reserves before any conflicting action might be taken in reserve officer promotion provisions.[25]

A key question by Senator Margaret Chase Smith met this argument head on and apparently created an atmosphere of acceptance for the bill as it was. When Senator

Smith asked Dr. Hannah if his "New Look" bill for a revised reserve system would include anything on retirement pay or promotion for reserve officers, the reply was that the plan would *not* have any such provisions. Senator Smith then concluded that action on H.R. 6573 could not create any inconsistencies.[26]

Despite an appeal from President Eisenhower to delay action on the bill until a complete revision of the reserve system could be prepared for legislative consideration in 1955, the Senate passed the bill without opposition. In partial deference to the President's request, the effective date of the bill was changed to July 1, 1955, to allow for additional considerations that a revised reserve program might suggest. The House concurred.[27] Almost a year was then available to the services to devise a system of implementation for ROPA. If amendments were required to clarify the Act, time would then be available to handle them before the Act went into effect.

PERFECTING AMENDMENTS OF 1955

Requests for clarifying and procedural amendments as well as some substantive changes in ROPA were made by the ROA and the NGA before the law was to become effective. Senator Margaret Chase Smith responded to the ROA's request for changes in 1955 by introducing S. 1718, which sought to protect those officers of the reserve components who might be eliminated from service for failure to be promoted with less than two years left to qualify for retirement.[28] After a careful determination of ROPA's impact on the Air National Guard, the National Guard Association requested changes in the Air National Guard category that were designed to exempt flying personnel from being brought under the mandatory promotion provision and pushed out of a unit that could not provide unit positions for those promoted.[29] Several other substantive changes and a series of clarifying and procedural amendments were also added.

There was no opposition to the amendments. At both Senate and House hearings, the Assistant Secretary of the Navy acted as the agent for the Department of Defense and the separate services in giving approval to the perfecting amendments, although he indicated that the Defense Department would not have sought changes of its own account until it had had experience in administering the law. In its course through both houses, S. 1718 passed without objection and became law just two days before ROPA went into effect on July 1, 1955.[30]

NEW DIMENSIONS ACQUIRED

The passage of the Reserve Officer Personnel Act of 1954 and its clarifying amendments marked the achievement of another major segment of a comprehensive armed forces reserve program. Finally imbedded in statute was a system of promotion for reserve officers differing slightly from service to service but providing for considerations of promotion and retention at specified times. Precedence and service for promotion was credited on the basis of satisfactory inactive duty training as well as active duty service, just as the reserve retirement plan had done in 1948. Channels of promotion were thus established for reservists on both active and inactive duty.

An analysis of this example of legislative policy-making adds another dimension to the pattern of Congressional activity in this area. The influence of the Reserve Officers Association was greatly expanded during the deliberation on this bill; the work of the ROA placed it near the National

Guard Association as one of the two foremost military associations helping to forge reserve policy. A tribute to the work of the ROA as it kept pressing for a statutory promotion system for reserve officers was made by the Republican Chairman of the House Armed Services subcommittee dealing with reserve forces, Representative Leroy Johnson, in his remarks at the hearing on the ROPA amendments:

> I don't think we can thank these two gentlemen [Colonels Boyer and Chambers of the ROA] enough for the work they did and for helping to bring passage of that bill [ROPA]. If we get the amendments through now the bill will spell out and do exactly what the ROA had in mind.[31]

In the future, Congress could not afford to listen any more closely to the National Guard Association than to the Reserve Officers Association. The strength of the ROA can also be gauged by the opposition it overcame in guiding ROPA through the legislative process. Strong pleadings from the Department of Defense and the services backed up by the NGA were not sufficient to block ROA recommendations from being embodied in the law. As a compromise Congress established July 1, 1955, as the effective date for ROPA so that the administration could propose amendments at the next session and have a fair chance of getting them accepted before the effective date.

Here was another demonstration of the importance of a small group of legislative specialists, including congressmen, professional committee staff, and representatives from the military associations, in handling complex statutory policy-making. Other congressmen tended to defer to that expertise in the absence of any great public sentiment against it. In the case of reserve affairs we find strong influences generated by subcommittees acting as powerful Congressional domains. Change of control from one party to the other had no perceptible effect on the attitude of the subcommittee toward reserve forces legislation. There was no break in the continuity of policy-making between 1952 and 1953 or between 1954 and 1955. Even the plea of the President failed to halt the action of members of his party in making a committee decision to act on a bill.

As a major participating team in the legislative policy-making process, the Department of Defense did not choose to make an all-out effort in pressing for its position in a concerted manner. Perhaps it did not want to risk such a conflict with a Congress sympathetic to the reserve position. The Defense Department did not exert the same positive action on the Reserve Officer Personnel Act that it displayed in the Reserve Acts of 1952 and 1955 because it was not ready to act on the matter. Basically, the decision of Congress to place personnel regulations into statutory form was consistent with Congressional rationale of conducting close executive supervision.

The Reserve Officer Personnel Act was regarded by federal reserve component officers as part of an over-all personnel policy that would put them on an equal footing with the regular establishment. Since it was expected that a significant part of military manpower requirements for a slightly modified foreign policy of containment could be met with reserve forces, the program established under ROPA would make a substantial contribution to the development of a continuing reservoir of personnel in the officer category. The Defense Department was not willing to concede at this early date that ROPA was an essential feature of the reserve program, but it was also somewhat less than fully motivated to oppose it.

In the next chapter we shall consider an example of Congressional oversight in the armed forces reserve policy area. Both the Army National Guard and the Army Reserve were faced with an executive-directed reduction in paid-drill strength during the last three years of the Eisenhower administration. How the decision on reserve manpower levels was handled in Congress will provide another illustration of the pattern of legislative policy-making for reserve forces.

Footnotes

1. House Committee on Armed Services, *Reserve Officer Personnel Act*, H. Rept. 1026 to accompany H.R. 6573, 83d Cong., 1st sess., 1953, p. 3.

2. 66 *Stat.* 486, Section 216a (1952).

3. 61 *Stat.* 795 (1947). In 1960, greater uniformity of standards for the appointment, promotion, and separation of officers of all the armed services was proposed by a committee headed by retired Army General Charles Bolté. The so-called Bolté bill was introduced in both the 88th and the 89th congresses but has yet to be passed. In its present form the Bolté proposal would abolish ROPA promotions for career active duty reservists and thus prevent them from retiring at a reserve grade possibly higher than the one in which reservists serve on active duty. See *Journal of the Armed Forces*, CII (March 27, 1965), 16–17 and *Officer*, XLII (May, 1965), 5.

4. House Committee on Armed Services, *Hearings, Reserve Officer Personnel Act*, H.R. 1222 83d Cong., 1st sess., 1953, p. 1983.

5. "Further Study Slated for Gray Board Report," *Army and Navy Journal*, LXXXV (August 14, 1948), 1403.

6. House Committee on Armed Services, *Hearings, Reserve Officer Personnel Act*, H.R. 1222, 83d Cong., 1st sess., 1953, p. 1612.

7. *Congressional Record*, 83d Cong., 2d sess., 1954, p. 14953.

8. Charles M. Boyer, "Convention Text Report," *Reserve Officer*, XXIX (August, 1953), 25.

9. *Congressional Record*, 83d Cong., 2d sess., 1954, p. 246. It is interesting to note that a Democratic congressman introduced the bill developed in the Department of Defense under a Democratic administration just prior to its exit from office to a Republican-controlled Congress.

10. House Committee on Armed Services, *Hearings, Reserve Officer Personnel Act*, H.R. 1222, 83d Cong., 1st sess., 1953, pp. 1527–54.

11. House Committee on Armed Services, *Hearings, Reserve Officer Personnel Act,* H.R. 1222, 83d Cong., 1st sess., 1953, pp. 1600, 1607, 1612–20.

12. "On Capitol Hill," *Reserve Officer,* XXIX (July, 1953), 7. The numbers requested were: Army, 275,000; Navy, 275,000 (25,000 Marines); Air Force, 275,000; and Coast Guard, 12,500.

13. House Committee on Armed Services, *Hearings, Reserve Officer Personnel Act,* H.R. 1222, 83d Cong., 1st sess., 1953, pp. 2044, 2064, 2069. In the Navy's running mate system each Naval reserve officer is assigned a corresponding officer in the regular service with corresponding or equivalent service. The reserve officer is then considered for promotion at the same time the regular officer is considered.

14. *Ibid.,* pp. 1558, 1561, 1583, 2037.

15. Colonel Charles M. Boyer, then Executive Director of the ROA, thought that frequently the turnover of service personnel and of civilian chiefs in the Defense Department put the Department at a disadvantage compared with experienced congressmen at the subcommittee and representatives from the military associations. (Interview conducted on March 24, 1964, in Washington, D.C.)

16. House Committee on Armed Services, *Hearings, Reserve Officer Personnel Act,* H.R. 1222, 83d Cong., 1st sess., 1953, pp. 2072–77.

17. *Congressional Record,* 83d Cong., 1st sess., 1953, pp. 10687–91.

18. "Reserve Officers Association Washington News Letter," *Reserve Officer,* XXIX (September, 1953), 1.

19. See notes 34 and 35 of Chapter III, *supra.*

20. Senate Committee on Armed Services, *Hearings, Reserve Officer Personnel Act of 1954,* H.R. 6573, 83d Cong., 2d sess., 1954, pp. 3–4.

21. *Ibid.,* p. 26.

22. Colonel Charles M. Boyer continued in his role as co-ordinator of the Reserve Officers Association presentations. Major General Melvin Maas returned with a strong appeal. Newly-elected President of the Association, Strom Thurmond, made an impressive case judging from Committee reaction, and Colonel Joseph Chambers, a Congressional Medal of Honor winner, came in as Deputy Executive Director of the Association.

23. Senate Committee on Armed Services, *Hearings, Reserve Officer Personnel Act of 1954,* H.R. 6573, 83d Cong., 2d sess., 1954, p. 177.

24. *Ibid.*, pp. 117, 137, 141–42.

25. *Ibid.*, pp. 167–68.

26. *Ibid.*, p. 178.

27. *Congressional Record*, 83d Cong., 2d sess., 1954, pp. 14953, 15235.

28. Senate Committee on Armed Services, *Hearings, Amendments to the Reserve Officer Personnel Act of 1954*, S. 1718, 84th Cong., 1st sess., 1955, pp. 1–2.

29. *Ibid.*, pp. 29–36.

30. *Congressional Record*, 84th Cong., 1st sess., 1955, pp. 9407–9.

31. House Committee on Armed Services, *Subcommittee Hearings on S. 1718*, Committee Paper No. 21, 84th Cong., 1st sess., 1955, p. 4097.

5

RESERVE FORCE LEVELS
Attempts to Reduce Paid-Drill Strength

5

RESERVE FORCE LEVELS
Attempts to Reduce Paid-Drill Strength

HOPES for continued growth of the reserve components of the Army, sparked by provisions of the legislation already analyzed in this study, were dimmed temporarily between 1958 and 1960. Danger signals came from budget proposals in each of these years calling for a 10 per cent reduction in the paid-drill strength of the Army Reserve and the Army National Guard.[1] This administration-directed effort was significant for national security because it represented a reversal of the trend to expand reserve forces and because it affected them in the categories of greatest readiness. Numerically, these two components comprised about three-fourths of the paid-drill strength of all reserve components; and politically, they were probably the most sensitive to any efforts to cut strength.[2]

MAJOR THEMES AND FORCES INVOLVED

Four themes dominated the legislative response to attempts by the President to reduce the paid-drill strength of the Army reserve components between 1958 and 1960. First, there was Congressional resentment over the continued erosion of its role in military policy-making by executive branch initiative. Formulation and direction of military policy have tended to fall to the executive branch, since military policy is a vital element of the President's unquestioned responsibility for the conduct of foreign affairs. To compensate for this change of balance in favor of executive power, Congress has influenced military policy-making by focusing its oversight and appropriation functions on that process. The issue of reserve force strength involved one of the instruments of military policy and provided an opportunity for Congress to make an adjustment in the balance of power in its favor.

Second, with a pervading goal to reduce federal expenditures, the administration saw reserve forces as an appropriate item for budget-cutting. The evaluation of Army reserve components by the Defense Department, the National Security Council, the Bureau of the Budget, and the President did not place these components in a favorable position for fund requests in comparison with missile procurement and active-duty personnel needs. This judgment was based on the strategy that more reliance should be placed on nuclear retaliatory striking power for sufficient deterrent and on professional military personnel for the maintenance of limited war capabilities.

Third, doubts were raised about the need for a large mobilization base of citizen-soldiers under such a revised strategy. However, there was a danger that removing the citizen from any obligation to share in the preparation for defense of the country might encourage him to underestimate the implications of American military commitments. Since most Americans have accepted the idea that military service is a duty of citizenship, reliance solely on a professional military force would tend to undermine this tradition.

Fourth, the competitive spirit between the Army Reserve and the National Guard prevented their allied associations from working together closely to block the threatened reduction in both components. Defense of each component's authorized strength level sometimes revealed the strong points of one at the expense of the other.

Setting policy on force levels through the appropriations process provides another illustration of Congressional decision-making in the armed forces reserve area. Although there had been a tendency for Congress to defer to the executive on such decisions as force levels since 1946, at least for the regular services, Congress chose to remain firm in its attempt to compel the executive branch to maintain a higher level of reserve forces than it had requested.[3] The nature of Congressional determination to maintain the strength of the reserve forces can be seen from this remark by the Chairman of the House Armed Services Reserve Subcommitte at the time:

> If the powers in the Pentagon think they are going to destroy the Reserve program they are ripe for another thought. Congress is going to demand that they answer for it, and my committee is expecting those answers to begin early in this session of Congress.[4]

From an administration viewpoint the proposal to reduce the strength of the Army reserve components in 1958 was designed to fulfil budgetary and strategic objectives in the service departments. In the spring of that year total expenditures for all government operations were running $2.5 billion higher than the budget estimate. When planned force levels for regular components were revised downward, attention was also drawn to the reserve components as a possible place for reduction in the budget for the following year.[5] It was questioned whether the reserve components were an economical substitute for reductions in active duty forces. There were also serious doubts about the efficacy of a strategy of mobilization encouraging a large reserve force. A reduction in the number and an upgrading in readiness of reservists on pay status were parts of what became known as the "New New Look" in American defense planning. Guardsmen and reservists saw this reduction as the first step toward eventual elimination of civilian components from contingency war planning.

The debate in the reserve area uncovered disagreements over the assumptions, the wisdom, and the means of implementing the new strategy. Critics of the strategy would not accept the implicit assumption that a reduction in Soviet-American tensions during the second Eisenhower term did in any way reduce Soviet military capability. Their contention was that American capability must be prepared to meet Soviet capability—rather than perceived Soviet intentions. Although it was accepted that economic considerations must be a part of determining what resources should be devoted to military forces, it was not agreed that they should be the dominant factor. There were also suggestions from those sympathetic with the reserve view that the manner of implementing the new strategy did not require any reduction in reserve forces in order to change the emphasis to other elements of the national defense strategy. Active forces could be increased in number while the reserve force levels remained steady. In these ways the proposed reduction of paid-drill strength in the reserve components of the Army was enmeshed in the over-all changes attempted in national strategy.

Although both the Army National Guard and the Army Reserve were threatened with a reduction in strength, the military associations representing each group were not able

to restrain component rivalry enough to adopt a close working relationship on this issue. The National Guard Association bristled with indignation because the proposed 10 per cent reduction in each component tended to put both components on the same plane. It suggested that the House Armed Services Reserve Subcommittee might well look into the Army policy, which intended to push the National Guard strength *down* to 400,000 while trying to pull the Reserve strength *up* to 300,000.[6]

The Reserve Officers Association represented Army Reserve interests primarily but it also included the National Guard in its defense of civilian components. Part of this was probably due to tactics adapted to the situation, since the National Guard Association undoubtedly wielded greater political influence. The emphasis in this matter will be placed on the Army Reserve and the Reserve Officers Association because it is consistent with the emphasis of the entire study on the reserve components under exclusive federal control as distinguished from the National Guard.

PREPARATION OF DEFENSE BUDGET PROPOSALS

Before a departmental budget reaches Congress, it is subjected to intensive review by many units both within and outside of the department. Budgeting within the Department of Defense for a reduction in Army reserve component strength would affect three reserve accounts primarily: (1) personnel, (2) operations and maintenance, and (3) construction.[7] Consideration of funds for these accounts necessarily involves the Bureau of the Budget whose advice on fiscal policy must be considered, if not accepted. Agencies participating in the determination of national strategy such as the National Security Council are also involved in budget deliberations. Within the Department of Defense extensive co-ordination is carried out between sections directly responsible for reserve planning, the general staff of each service, the Secretary of the service, the Joint Chiefs of Staff, and officials of the Defense Department's highest echelon, including the Secretary. Special processing unique to the Department of Defense in contrast to other departments is a joint review of the budget proposals with the Bureau of the Budget.[8] After the joint review any remaining differences over major items are then resolved by the President before the entire budget is submitted to Congress.

Within this framework the Director of the Bureau of the Budget moved very carefully in the preparation of budget proposals in 1958 for the fiscal year 1959. He denied setting any ceilings for the defense budget for fiscal 1959, but he recommended that the Department of Defense begin with an over-all expenditure of desirable magnitude based on anticipated revenue. The Defense Department could then determine the type of defense it could provide for that amount of money and decide whether it was an adequate program.[9]

For the fiscal 1959 budget, broad guidance for defense planning was supplied by the National Security Council through its annual Basic National Security Policy. From this the Joint Chiefs of Staff developed the Joint Strategic Objective Plan, which provided the planning guidance for the determination of such matters as force levels and matériel procurement. The Joint Chiefs of Staff also worked out estimates of military requirements for force levels in each service that would be capable of executing the missions deduced from the national defense policy.[10]

Within the Department of the Army, the Chief of Staff, operating in his service capacity, co-ordinated recommendations for Army Reserve force levels. The Deputy Chief of

Staff for Military Oeprations, the Chief of Army Reserve and ROTC, and the Chief of the National Guard Bureau developed estimates of funds needed for that part of over-all Army requirements to be fulfilled by the reserve components.[11] During this period of consideration, advice was offered by the General Staff Committee on Army Reserve Policy.[12] With these estimates and recommendations, the Army Chief of Staff, the Secretary of the Army, and his civilian staff put together an Army budget for submission to the Secretary of Defense. In 1958 the Department of Army budget proposal did not call for a 10 per cent reduction in paid-drill strength of the reserve components.

It was really at the Department of Defense echelon where service programs for fiscal 1959 met their first serious tests. At this point recommendations on such a matter as reserve force strengths came from the Reserve Forces Policy Board, the Joint Chiefs of Staff, and the Assistant Secretary of Defense for Manpower and Reserves. An Army request for fiscal 1959 to support 300,000 paid-drill reservists had to be considered within the framework of all defense forces before the Secretary of Defense made the final decision. In this case he chose to lower the fund requests by amounts that would bring a 10 per cent reduction in the Army reserve components' paid-drill strength.[13]

The reaction of Army reserve component members to this proposed reduction in paid-drill strength was formed as other pressures were being placed on them at about the same time. A major reorganization plan based on the pentomic division concept was introduced to the Army reserve components in March, 1958.[14] Its objectives were to reduce the number of units and to change the type of many units remaining so as to accommodate the needs of modern combat conditions for increased mobility and firepower. In addition, appropriated funds for the construction of armories were not being apportioned by the Bureau of the Budget because the long-range reserve strength was in doubt in the latter part of 1957.

Reservists on extended active duty also experienced cutbacks. A reduction in the Active Forces affected many reservists who had been on extended active duty since World War II and were only several years short of qualifying for retirement pay. The heavy response to the Reserve Forces Act of 1955 by six-month trainees began to strain the facilities of the regular establishment to the point that the program had to be temporarily halted.[15] Of less direct effect on reserve affairs at this time was the legislative proposal to reorganize the Department of Defense, placing the Joint Chiefs in the chain of field command under the Secretary of Defense. Here the National Guard Bureau feared that it might lose its statutory position. From the perspective of all these pressures, the proposed 10 per cent reduction in the Army reserve components' paid-drill strength was part of a composite picture of an attempted deemphasis of the reserve forces.

STRENGTH REDUCTION PROPOSALS
FACE CONGRESSIONAL TESTS

Once the administration's budget was submitted to Congress, the responsibility to justify its provisions rested with each department or agency. In most cases at appropriations hearings, agency officials present evidence for fund requests that Congress initially regards as too high. However, for reserve force appropriations the converse was frequently true. In 1958 military and civilian officials found themselves in a position of trying to justify appropriation requests for the reserve components of the Army for amounts *less* than Congress regarded as adequate. At the hearings of the

House Appropriations Defense Subcommittee, headed by George Mahon, the request for fiscal 1959 for Army Reserve personnel of $185 million was $18 million less than the amount for the previous year and was capable of supporting a strength no greater than 270,000 on paid-drill status, a reduction of 30,000 in that category.[16]

Since the Mahon subcommittee tended to view Defense Department recommendations for the Army Reserve and the Army National Guard with considerable skepticism, a searching analysis was made of the budgetary items for both components. Who made the proposals for a 10 per cent reduction in paid-drill strength? Who developed the budgetary justifications in support of them? The subcommittee sought to pinpoint the responsibility for such action.

Both Secretary of the Army Wilber Brucker and Army Chief of Staff General Maxwell Taylor admitted that they had originally recommended a paid-drill strength of 300,000 for the Army Reserve and 400,000 for the National Guard but that these numbers were reduced by 10 per cent at the Department of Defense level.[17] Other military officials responsible for administering the programs for the two Army civilian components agreed that strength reduction directives came from the Secretary of Defense.[18] Justification for the proposed reductions in Army reserve component strength was based on an extensive review of the reserve program in the light of the international situation, the need for maximum return from defense spending, and the changing concepts of war. Reorganization of the Active Army along pentomic lines gave it greater flexibility, firepower, and effectiveness. A similar reorganization was planned for the reserve components because it offered the same advantages with a slight reduction in personnel.[19] Readiness to respond quickly with well-trained reserve components rather than a large mobilization base fitted into the pattern of deterrence.

As the disagreement between the Department of the Army and the Department of Defense was being examined in Congressional hearings, the Army Reserve indicated the manner in which its recommendation for 300,000 could be implemented. Its total strength in February, 1958, of 253,000 was projected to 291,000 before restrictions were placed on recruiting. With an additional $52 million in funds, paid-drill strength could be increased to the desired 300,000.[20] The growth capacity of the Army Reserve was further illustrated by these remarks of its Chief: "While we are frequently associated with the long historical tradition of the citizen soldier we are in fact young, very young, but nevertheless a growing giant suffering growing pains."[21]

In their appearances before the House Armed Services Subcommittee on Reserve Components, civilian and military officials from the Pentagon continued to reveal the disagreement over what constituted adequate reserve force strength between the Department of the Army and the Department of Defense. However, Secretary Brucker and General Taylor accepted the final 10 per cent reduction and made no pleas to reverse the recommendation.[22] It was a very delicate position for the Army to uphold a decision with which it did not agree and to acknowledge that its own recommendations were at variance with the Department of Defense. One of the key points around which the disagreement centered was whether a lower manning level was adequate for the state of readiness required for mobilization under modern conditions. Since the matter was one primarily of appropriations, the House Armed Services subcommittee approached the matter by giving serious consideration to resolutions expressing approval for a 300,000-man Army Reserve and a force of 400,000 for the Army National Guard. There was the possibility that such resolutions might be embodied in the provisions of the appropriations bill.

MILITARY ASSOCIATIONS FIGHT PROPOSED
REDUCTIONS

Although members of both the Reserve Officers Association and the National Guard Association were indirectly under attack from the Department of Defense, on roughly similar grounds, they did not combine forces in the effort to defeat the proposed reduction in reserve component strength of the Army. The ROA mobilized resources of impressive quality, but certainly of less quantity than those used by the NGA to fight the reduction.

President of the ROA deLesseps Morrison, at the time a reserve brigadier general and Mayor of New Orleans, was one of the few who pleaded for both components. However, his rather broad indictment of the Pentagon for "unduly restricting" the reserve program caused some anxiety among friends of the Army Reserve in the Department of the Army.[23] General Morrison felt that provisions should have been made for a more extensive training program to include a greater number of enlisted personnel. Although the Army Reserve Chief was eager to form strong opposition to a proposed reduction in Army Reserve strength, he was not willing to accept General Morrison's remarks in full because they reflected on his administration of the program.[24]

Another resource used by the Reserve Officers Association in the fight against the strength reduction proposal was its Legislative Advisory Committee, made up of ten congressmen who were also reservists and members of the ROA. This group was led by Congressman LeRoy Anderson of Montana, holder of a brilliant combat record in World War II and, in 1958, the Commanding General of the Ninety-sixth Infantry Division of the Army Reserve. His review of the reserve program before the Brooks Subcommittee was impressive for its military background and for its emphasis on how reservists brought understanding of defense needs to their communities. He thought that the Army Reserve could meet any strength goal that the national policy would support, but he hoped it would be a minimum of 300,000 in paid-drill strength.[25]

The ROA also effectively obtained support from three other areas through Major General L. J. Sverdrup. Just recently retired as the commander of the 102d Infantry Division (Reserve) centered in St. Louis, General Sverdrup brought backing from the Senior Reserve Commanders Association as its President, from the General Staff Committee on National Guard and Army Reserve Policy, and from the Reserve Forces Policy Board. The latter two governmental advisory groups passed unanimously, with all members participating, resolutions strongly objecting to the proposed cuts in reserve strength.[26]

Although the action of National Guard elements is not of direct concern, undoubtedly some of the support mobilized by them helped the Army Reserve cause. This occurred despite some resentment that the proposed reduction of 40,000 spaces in the Guard would have been an actual loss of personnel, whereas the 30,000-man cut in the Army Reserve represented only programmed strength rather than actual strength.[27] Suggestions that the Guard was not in any higher state of readiness than the Army Reserve piqued Guard leaders. Through the Governors' Conference all forty-eight states were recorded in opposition to the proposed cut in the Guard.[28] Reinforcing that stand was the unanimous action of the Adjutants General Association opposing the Pentagon proposal to trim National Guard forces to 360,000.[29] Early in 1958, the National Guard Association convened its committees on Legislation and Army Affairs to plan an intensive campaign against cuts in Guard strength. It began with a letter to President Eisenhower.[30]

Later, within the Pentagon and Congressional circles, National Guard Major Generals Edgar C. Erickson and Donald McGowan made clear their opposition concerning the personnel cut.

TWO ANSWERS EMERGE FROM CONGRESS

There was no doubt that the House would oppose the attempt to reduce the strength of the Army's reserve components. The only question was the manner in which it would express its disagreement. The answers came in the form of restored appropriations and in the form of directions to use them to maintain reserve component strength. The Armed Services Committee requested that the Army National Guard be maintained at an average yearly strength of 400,000 and that the Army Reserve be maintained at an average strength of 300,000.[31] Although the House Appropriations Committee did add sufficient funds to the budget to restore these civilian component force levels, it did not add the provisos to the defense appropriations bill, H.R. 12738, that specific strengths *had* to be maintained.[32] In this form the House passed it unanimously.

Members of the House Armed Services Committee then secured a House concurrent resolution to assure a paid-drill strength of 400,000 for the Army National Guard.[33] There were several reasons that this resolution did not include the Army Reserve, and they reflect differences in the effectiveness of Guard and Reserve support. In 1957 a memorandum of understanding was negotiated between the Army, the National Guard, and the House Armed Services Committee in which the Army agreed to maintain the National Guard strength at 400,000, and, in return, the National Guard agreed to accept the provision that all its members had to complete at least six months of active-duty training.[34] The proposal to reduce that strength by 10 per cent in the fiscal year 1959 was regarded as a repudiation of that agreement and as reason for the need of greater assurance on strength maintenance. It was further pointed out that the Guard matter had come up differently through the governors and the Adjutants General Association and that the Guard had been suffering greater actual losses than the Army Reserve. Each House member was reminded that he had at least one or more National Guard units in his own district.[35]

At this point the Reserve Officers Association was not able to secure enough support for a similar resolution for the Army Reserve. Congressman Anderson had raised this question from the floor, but no resolution was offered. This was a good indication of the subtle difference in political effectiveness between the National Guard Association and the Reserve Officers Association, although in this case the final result was not affected by the difference.

Secretary of Defense Neil McElroy carried the administration's case for a reduction in Army reserve component strength to the Senate Armed Services Committee by suggesting that even more drastic reductions were under consideration in the year ahead.[36] After hearing much of the same testimony from the Army Reserve Office and the National Guard Bureau that was given in the House, the Senate wanted greater assurance that the strength of the Army's reserve components would be maintained without change. Its Committee on Appropriations added funds for the Army Reserve and the National Guard and incorporated House Concurrent Resolution 333, which guaranteed the Guard strength, into its appropriation recommendations.[37] Governor Joe Foss of South Dakota kept watch on the Senate proceedings for the Governors' Conference as head of its special subcommittee for the appropriations bill.[38] Congressman LeRoy Anderson tried to secure a similar assurance for a minimum paid-drill strength of 300,000 for the Army Reserve from the Senate Appropriations Committee, but he was unsuccessful. Only on the floor, by amendment to the appropriations bill for defense, was Senator Strom Thurmond able to achieve that result. In contrast to the original budget request from President Eisenhower, funds for the Army reserve components were raised, and provisos requiring a minimum paid-drill strength were added by legislative action.[39]

The final form of the Defense Appropriations Act of 1959 thus represented a larger budget for reserve forces than the administration preferred.[40] President Eisenhower made clear his displeasure at having to accept the proviso on the maintenance of minimum strength levels for the Army Reserve and the National Guard, which he characterized as "an unprecedented departure from past policy."[41] Estimates by the National Guard of what it took to establish the "unprecedented" were labeled as "the most impressive array of support since the enactment of the National Defense Act of 1916."[42] The Reserve Officers Association did not claim a great victory because the strength of the Army Reserve was assured for only one more year.[43] Perhaps there was good reason for the insistence on the inclusion of a provision for minimum paid-drill strength in the Appropriations Act if actions by the Bureau of the Budget shortly after its passage can be used as a criterion. Army and Marine Corps strength in the active forces was to be trimmed by a freeze of funds.[44] If special assurance in legislation had not been sought to maintain Army reserve component strengths, a somewhat similar withholding of funds might have faced them. As it was, there was some question about whether the provisos would have to be invoked before the end of the fiscal year.

Both Army reserve components had to work hard to secure personnel for their desired strength. During fiscal 1959 the Army Reserve came close to fulfilling its authorized goal. Its assigned paid strength was 302,000 by December 31, 1958,[45] and 294,771 by the end of the fiscal year.[46] The National Guard failed to maintain an average strength of 400,000 because money for the needed six-month trainees was not released until late in the fiscal year. Only with great recruiting efforts was the Guard able to climb back to 400,000 by the end of fiscal 1959.[47] Assistant Secretary of Defense for Manpower, Personnel, and Reserves, Charles Finucane, indicated that the Guard should have worked harder to recruit prior-service personnel to fill its quotas early in the fiscal year so that it would not have had to rely on recruits needing six months of training.[48]

THE "UNPRECEDENTED" BECOMES THE USUAL

Since 1958 the paid-drill strength of the two reserve components of the Army has been a matter of contention between the Department of Defense, joined by the Bureau of the Budget on one side, and the reserve component offices in the Department of the Army, the Reserve Officers Association, and the National Guard Association on the other, with Congress backing the latter grouping. For each of the next three fiscal years (1960–62), 10 per cent reductions in the paid-drill strength of the two components were proposed in the departmental budget, and such recommendations were revised by the appropriation acts. The Department of Defense offered the improved state of readiness and training prevailing among Army reserve components as a reason for requiring less personnel in paid training; it indicated that the number of men on reserve status no longer had the significance it once had.[49] For fiscal 1960 and 1961 guarantees of Guard strength continued to be included in the appropriations legislation.[50]

For the Army Reserve in fiscal 1960 and 1961, instead of a guarantee of strength such as it had given the Guard, the Defense Department merely pledged to maintain the Army Reserve without reduction in strength. The Reserve Officers Association thought that such a pledge to abide by the decision of Congress would become just as binding as a statutory proviso for that purpose. The ROA felt it had sufficient influence to exact enforcement of the pledge if the executive branch tried to circumvent it. Its success with the Reserve Acts of 1952 and 1955, the Reserve Officer Personnel Act, and previous budget actions was the basis for its confidence in this expectation. Less effort was needed to secure a pledge that the funds would be used. If there was hesitation to fulfil the pledge, then any energy that would have been expended for getting a statutory guarantee was still available to seek enforcement of the pledge. No doubt the statutory provision requiring a minimum strength for a reserve component was a greater assurance that the strength would be maintained, but in practice it was not really needed.[51]

Upon the return of the units from the Berlin mobilization, a different type of proviso was added to the appropriation acts dealing with the two Army reserve components for the fiscal years 1963–65. The Secretary of Defense agreed to program for a drill pay strength of 300,000 for the Army Reserve and 400,000 for the Army National Guard. Programming for this strength meant moving as quickly as possible toward these strength goals as long as certain conditions of readiness were maintained within the paid-drill units.[52] However, actual strength has never reached the programmed goals. At the end of fiscal 1964, the Army Reserve had an actual paid-drill strength of 268,000 and was budgeted for 285,000.[53] For fiscal 1965, the budget provided for only 285,000 in Army Reserve drill strength—

the amount believed to be attainable—but the programming was for 300,000.[54] Although guidelines established by the Secretary of Defense, as well as certain restrictions placed on the allocation of appropriations, acted as a brake to some extent in moving toward the programmed strength in each of these years, it is probable that neither the Army Reserve nor the Army National Guard would have been able to recruit or retain in the reserve components any more personnel than the strength actually attained. The programmed strength probably reflected the maximum expectation of reserve component recruiting and retention efforts under entirely favorable conditions. Evidence of intensive recruiting activity in the Army Reserve tends to confirm this conclusion.[55] Annual turnover rates in recent years approach 30 per cent, so most of the recruiting effort merely replaces the losses.[56]

Despite the difficulties observed in bringing the actual strength up to the level of authorized and programmed strengths in the reserve components of the Army, with the exception of fiscal 1961, programmed strengths have remained almost constant and have been specified for one or both reserve components of the Army in the appropriation acts.[57] Actual strengths have been affected by two major reorganization plans, the pentomic concept in 1958–59 and the ROAD concept in 1962–63, by the Berlin recall, and by high turnover rates.[58] The proposal in 1958 to reduce the authorized strength of the Army reserve components by 10 per cent was *symbolic* rather than extensive. If the reduction had been sustained, it would have indicated the political capability to limit the role of the citizen-soldier. Further reductions probably would have followed. The authorized strengths of the two Army reserve components were officially accepted quantitative definitions of what that role should be. The executive branch could have achieved actual reduction without such a fight to reduce programmed strengths merely by letting high attrition rates cause a decrease in actual strength levels.

The most recent proposal by the Secretary of Defense to reduce paid-drill strength of the Army reserve components by merging the Army Reserve into the National Guard is both *symbolic and extensive.* It would amount to a major limitation on the role of the citizen-soldier, a transfer of considerable operational authority for national defense preparations to the states, and a reduction in authorized paid-drill strength of about 150,000.[59] Although the proposal is more drastic than any previous ones, its early chances of success seemed better because it was more politically attuned to reality. Instead of arousing the opposition of both components, it makes an appeal to the component with the greatest political influence, the National Guard. The eventual outcome is considered in greater detail in the last three chapters.

SUMMARY OF THE PROCESS

Paid-drill strength for Army reserve components was an extremely favorable issue for a Congress desirous of exercising a primacy of interest in military policy-making. For Congress it meant fighting a battle on favorable terrain since it controlled the appropriations process. Essentially blocking an executive proposal to reduce reserve component paid-drill strength was a defensive action, and this is usually a position of advantage in the legislative process. It was extremely difficult to confine the issue to strictly budgetary or even strategic grounds because a controversy over the size of reserve forces arouses a host of emotional overtones attached to the minuteman tradition. The success of the proviso requesting the executive branch to use appropriations in a prescribed manner for the reserve forces was a victory for Congress. It was an action that President Eisenhower, with a reputation for not laboring very hard over the mobilization of Congressional support, accepted despite his personal protests. In addition, in an area of appropriations such as reserve affairs where Congress is more likely to raise rather than lower executive budget estimates, a requested reduction by the Department of Defense would require strong justification.

A political strategy that proposed to reduce both the Reserve and the National Guard of the Army at the same time was a poor choice by the administration. Each reserve component had a strong interest group, and this proposal incurred the opposition of both at the same time. The Reserve Officers Association and the National Guard Association were competitors in the reserve area, but the threat to both brought them closer together in opposition to the proposal than would otherwise have been the case.

Interest group activity in this case was probably more sophisticated than ever before in the application of organization resources to the military reserve area. The Legislative Advisory Committee of the Reserve Officers Association is slightly reminiscent of the National Rivers and Harbors Congress established by the Corps of Engineers. Members of this committee acted as agents of the ROA to block effectively a threat to the goals of the organization. Through the encouragement of the National Guard Association, the Governors' Conference took an active part in protecting the paid-drill strength of reserve forces.

The proviso in the appropriation acts requiring the maintenance of desired strength levels in the civilian components of the Army was a convenient index of the comparative influence of the Reserve Officers Association and the National Guard Association. The NGA was able to secure this guarantee more easily than the ROA in 1958 and succeeded in maintaining it in subsequent years when the ROA could not reach this additional goal. In the latter years, the ROA was probably practicing an economy of effort with the careful appraisal that securing the proviso would require the use of more of its resources than it could afford to expend.

Despite ten years of experience, the Department of Defense could still not count on commanding a unified effort of the three services when it entered the Congressional arena with a legislative proposal. There were serious confrontations between Army leaders and civilian officials at the Defense Department level on civilian component strengths, but as yet the executive branch was not able to confine these differences within its family. Occasionally they spilled over into the legislative process. To some extent, Congress and the two military associations (ROA and NGA) encouraged professional military leaders to carry their case to Congress when the decision within the military departments went against them. At best, civilian control of the military was fragmented in operation, but in this case it was blurred by the impossibility of separating military and civilian interests. In other areas of the legislative process, the interest of congressmen in one program frequently benefits a civilian segment of the nation. When Congress becomes the protagonist of military reserve forces, however, it abets a military interest and further fragments civilian control over the military.

Congressional success in this case represents something more than the restoration of paid-drill strength spaces for Army civilian components. If the proposed reduction had been approved, it would have been the beginning of the end of the citizen-soldier concept. It would have signaled Congressional willingness to give up the concept. Leading academic critics backed up the Defense Department's proposal.[60] Defense Secretary McNamara would now like to try another approach in limiting the role of the citizen-soldier. By cutting the reserve strength, he would place greater reliance on a professional active duty force.[61] In spite of the opponents of the citizen-soldier concept, the legislature has preserved it. Congress has been willing to use the unusual device of securing a pledge from the executive branch to save the concept. Its sympathies for the concept have removed Congress from the role of mediator between the separate services and the Department of Defense as it frequently was in other military affairs.[62]

Another problem usually handled in the reserve category was the development of officer training programs on college campuses. The manner in which Congress recently revised policy in this area will be the topic of the next chapter.

Footnotes

1. *Budget of the United States Government for the Fiscal Year Ending June 30, 1959* (Washington, D.C.: Government Printing Office, 1958), pp. 453–54.

2. Charles H. Donnelly, *United States Defense Policies in 1958*, House Document No. 227, 86th Cong., 1st sess., 1959, p. 80. The total paid-strength of the Army civilian components, including the Reserve and the National Guard, on June 30, 1958, was 716,166, while that of the Navy and Air Force Reserve combined was 260,818.

3. Samuel P. Huntington, *The Common Defense* (New York: Columbia University Press, 1961), pp. 139–40. Congressional powers of authorization and appropriation were originally designed to prevent the executive from maintaining military forces without popular support.

4. Overton Brooks quoted in deLesseps S. Morrison, "Opening for a 'David'," *Officer*, XXXIV (January, 1958), inside front cover. His remarks were made upon receipt of the ROA's Distinguished Service Citation.

5. Donnelly, *op. cit.*, p. 60.

6. *National Guardsman*, XII (January, 1958), inside front cover. The National Guard Association contended that since Guard strength was close to its authorized total of 400,000, a 10 per cent reduction would be an actual loss of personnel. In contrast, the Army Reserve

actual strength was at least 10 per cent below its authorized level of 300,000. If such a reduction were actually imposed, it would mean only an administrative adjustment rather than an actual loss of personnel. National Guard feeling was that the Army really wanted to get rid of the Guard in order to remove its political influence and to be able to concentrate on a wholly federal force, which it would control completely.

7. For a comparison with recent changes in defense budget planning see Charles J. Hitch, *Decision-Making for Defense* (Berkeley: University of California Press, 1965), pp. 30–39. These budget appropriation accounts are still used as the basis for presentation of the budget to Congress. However, figures for these accounts are now converted from nine major programs, for each of which the unifying factor is a common mission or set of purposes. As can be seen from the following list of the major programs, reserve components still form a distinct grouping as they do under budget appropriation accounts. The nine major programs for Department of Defense budgetary planning are: (1) Strategic Retaliatory Forces, (2) Continental Defense Forces, (3) General Purpose Forces, (4) Airlift and Sealift, (5) Reserve and Guard, (6) Research and Development, (7) General Support, (8) Retired Pay, and (9) Military Assistance.

8. Senate Committee on Armed Services, *Hearings, Major Defense Matters*, Part 2, 86th Cong., 1st sess., 1959, p. 238.

9. *Ibid.*, pp. 298, 317. Director of the Budget Maurice Stans denied that his Bureau was a policy-making group, although he indicated it had a considerable amount of influence and force in its recommendations. Mr. Stans also attended National Security Council meetings, and his Bureau had membership on the National Security Council Planning Board.

10. Maxwell D. Taylor, *The Uncertain Trumpet* (New York: Harper & Bros., 1959), pp. 20-21.

11. Department of Defense, *Annual Report of the Secretary of Defense on Reserve Forces, Fiscal Year 1953* (Washington, D.C., December 20, 1963), p. 3. The ROTC is now separate from the Army Reserve Office, so the second part of the title of the office has been dropped.

12. The committee consists of six Army Reserve general officers, seven regular general officers, and one reserve colonel as executive resident officer. This group usually holds joint meetings with the Army National Guard Policy Committee.

13. House Committee on Appropriations, *Hearings, Department of Defense Appropriations for 1959: Overall Policy Statements*, 85th Cong., 2d sess., 1958, pp. 245, 351.

14. W. H. Lawrence, "Army Offers Plan for Cutting the Guard," *New York Times*, April 1, 1958, p. 1.

15. House Committee on Appropriations, *Hearings, Department of Defense Appropriations for 1959: Department of the Army*, 85th Cong., 2d sess., 1958, p. 161.

16. *Ibid.*, pp. 9–10. Army National Guard fund requests were $29 million less than the previous year and capable of supporting no more than 360,000 personnel in paid-drill status. Democratic majority subcommittee members in order of their seniority after Mr. Mahon were: Harry R. Sheppard, Calif.; Robert L. F. Sikes, Fla.; W. F. Norrell, Ark.; Jamie L. Whitten, Miss.; George W. Andrews, Ala.; John J. Riley, S.C.; Daniel J. Flood, Pa.; Albert Thomas, Tex.; and Charles A. Boyle, Ill. On the Republican minority side in order of seniority were: Richard B. Wigglesworth, Mass.; Errett P. Scrivner, Kan.; Gerald R. Ford, Jr., Mich.; Edward T. Miller, Md.; Harold C. Ostertag, N.Y.; Hamer H. Budge, Idaho; and Melvin R. Laird, Wisc.

17. House, Committee on Appropriations, *Hearings, Department of Defense Appropriations for 1959: Overall Policy Statements*, 85th Cong., 2d sess., 1958, pp. 246, 351.

18. House Committee on Appropriations, *Hearings, Department of Defense Appropriations for 1959: Department of the Army*, 85th Cong., 2d sess., 1958, pp. 163, 290. Major General Ralph Palladino was immediately responsible for Army Reserve activities, and Major General Donald McGowan was Chief, Army Division, National Guard Bureau.

19. House Committee on Armed Services, *Hearings, Proposed Reduction in the Strength of the National Guard*, Committee Paper No. 77, 85th Cong., 2d sess., 1958, pp. 5636, 5866.

20. House Committee on Appropriations, Hearings, *Department of Defense Appropriations for 1959: Department of the Army*, 85th Cong., 2d sess., 1958, pp. 177, 199, 217. At this same point of time, the Army National Guard had a paid-drill strength of 404,601 to be reduced to 360,000 by the end of fiscal 1959.

21. Ralph A. Palladino, "We Started from Scratch," *Army Reservist*, IV (February, 1958), 5.

22. House Committee on Armed Services, *Hearings, Proposed Reduction in the Strength of the National Guard*, Committee Paper No. 77, 85th Cong., 2d sess., 1958, pp. 5636, 5866.

23. House Committee on Appropriations, *Hearings, Department of Defense Appropriations for 1959: Overall Policy Statements*, 85th Cong., 2d sess., 1958, pp. 603–5. Also *Army, Navy, Air Force Journal*, XCV (February 1, 1958), 643.

24. House Committee on Appropriations, *Hearings, Department of Defense Appropriations for 1959: Department of the Army*, 85th Cong., 2d sess., 1958, p. 164.

25. House, Committee on Armed Services, *Hearings, Proposed Reduction in the Strength of the National Guard,* Committee Paper No. 77, 85th Cong., 2d sess., 1958, p. 5790.

26. *Ibid.,* p. 5804. The General Staff Committee on National Guard and Army Reserve Policy has nineteen general officers including seven from the Regular Army, six from the Army National Guard, and six from the Army Reserve plus a resident officer from each of the two reserve components. The chairman is the senior civilian component officer. The Reserve Forces Policy Board consists of fourteen general and flag officers representing all regular and civilian components. Its chairman is a civilian. Both groups are statutory bodies acting in an advisory capacity.

27. *Ibid.,* p. 5665.

28. "Four Governors Decry Plan to Cut Guard," *New York Times,* March 4, 1958, p. 22.

29. "Guard Heads Oppose Pentagon over Cuts," *New York Times,* July 15, 1958, p. 17.

30. "Washington Report," *National Guardsman,* XII (February, 1958), 6.

31. House Committee on Armed Services, *Full Committee Consideration of Subcommittee No. 1 Resolutions Relating to National Guard and Reserves,* Committee Paper No. 74, 85th Cong., 2d sess., 1958, p. 5053.

32. House Committee on Appropriations, *Department of Defense Appropriation Bill, 1959,* H. Rept. 1830 to accompany H.R. 12738, 85th Cong., 2d sess., 1958, p. 35.

33. *Congressional Record,* 85th Cong., 2d sess., 1958, pp. 14487–91. It was Resolution No. 333.

34. Carl Vinson, Chairman of the House Armed Services Committee, was largely responsible for arranging the negotiations.

35. House Committee on Armed Services, *Expressing the Sense of the Congress with Respect to the Size of the Army National Guard,* H. Rept. 2199 to accompany H. Con. Res. 333, 85th Cong., 2d sess., 1958, p. 3.

36. Senate Committee on Appropriations, *Hearings, Department of Defense Appropriations for 1959,* H.R. 12738, 85th Cong., 2d sess., 1958, pp. 26, 262.

37. Senate Committee on Appropriations, *Department of Defense Appropriation Bill, 1959.* S. Rept. 1937 to accompany H.R. 12738, 85th Cong., 2d sess., 1958, pp. 6, 27.

38. Donnelly, *op. cit.*, pp. 29–30. United States involvement in the Middle Eastern crisis at this time undoubtedly made the Senate action easier.

39. *Congressional Record*, 85th Cong., 2d sess., 1958, pp. 15600–15601.

40. 72 *Stat.* 715 (1958); and House Committee on Appropriations, *Department of Defense Appropriation Bill, 1959*, H. Rept. 2503 (Conference Rept.) on H.R. 12738, 85th Cong., 2d sess., 1958, p. 6.

41. "Eisenhower Fears Defense 'Waste,'" *New York Times*, August 23, 1958, p. 5.

42. Major General Donald McGowan, "Minute Men in the Missile Age," *National Guardsman*, XII (November, 1958), 17. Also in the *Official Proceedings of the National Guard Association of the United States*, Annual Convention for 1958, the report of the Legislative Committee stated in part: "Never in recent years had we been confronted with such a determined effort on the part of the Pentagon to destroy the Army National Guard."

43. *Officer*, which is the Association magazine, failed to reveal any notice of special accomplishment for the action between July and December of 1958.

44. "U.S. to Hold Back Extra Arms Fund and Trim Forces," *New York Times*, September 12, 1958, p. 1.

45. House Committee on Appropriations, *Hearings, Department of Defense Appropriations for 1960: Manpower, Personnel, and Reserves*, Part 3, 86th Cong., 1st sess., 1959, p. 153.

46. Department of Defense, *Annual Report of the Secretary of Defense, July 1, 1959, to June 30, 1960* (Washington, D.C.: Government Printing Office, 1960), p. 383.

47. "Washington Report," *National Guardsman*, XIII (August, 1959), 12.

48. House Committee on Appropriations, *Hearings, Department of Defense Appropriations for 1960: Manpower, Personnel, and Reserves*, Part 3, 86th Cong., 1st sess., 1959, pp. 251–53.

49. *Ibid.*, p. 10. The position was presented by Deputy Assistant Secretary of Defense Stephen S. Jackson.

50. 73 *Stat.* 367 (1959); and 74 *Stat.* 339 (1960).

51. *Officer*, XXXV (March, 1959), 22. Rear Admiral Leon Jacobi, President of the Reserve Officers Association, reported that the ROA had known the doors to the Pentagon, the White House, and Congress were open to its representatives, but it now knew that its representatives were *within* these doors. *Ibid.*, XXXV (November, 1959), 2. A letter was sent out by the Army Chief of Staff to all major com-

mands on the occasion of the thirty-seventh anniversary of the ROA urging the encouragement of support for its activities.

52. 76 *Stat.* 319 (1962); 77 *Stat.* 255 (1963); and 78 *Stat.* 465 (1964). In moving to meet the strength goals recommended by Congress, the Secretary of Defense used the following guides: (1) 90 per cent of the authorized positions within each unit must be filled by personnel who actually meet the qualifications required of personnel in those positions ("MOS qualified" is the term used to designate this condition, meaning qualified for the military occupation specialty); (2) recruiting standards for reservists must be the same as those for the regular forces; and (3) except to accommodate reservists recently displaced by reorganization actions, units must not carry more personnel on their rolls than were actually authorized by the tables of organization.

53. Senate Committee on Appropriations, *Hearings, Department of Defense Appropriations for 1965: Military Personnel,* Part 2, H.R. 10939, 88th Cong., 2d sess., 1964, p. 120.

54. House Committee on Armed Services, *Hearings on Military Posture and H.R. 9637,* Committee Paper No. 36, 88th Cong., 2d sess., 1964, p. 7026. This was brought out in Secretary McNamara's testimony.

55. William H. McDonald, "Army-wide USAR Recruiting Conference Is Held," *Army Reserve Magazine,* X (March, 1964), 4.

56. House Committee on Appropriations, *Hearings, Department of Defense Appropriations for 1965: Military Personnel,* Part 1, 88th Cong., 2d sess., 1964, p. 123. The evidence was given by the current Chief of the Army Reserve, Major General W. J. Sutton. The need to recruit heavily to replace losses was made clear in the Guard earlier in 1957 when similar turnover rates existed. See House Committee on Armed Services, *Review of Reserve Program by Subcommittee No. 1,* 85th Cong., 1st sess., 1957, pp. 1364, 1375.

57. Authorized strengths reflect the total spaces assigned to drill units. They have usually been somewhat under the programmed strengths. Authorized strength represents the goal for actual strength, but it can be exceeded up to the limit of the programmed strength.

58. Pentomic divisions had five battle groups with a somewhat fixed composition. ROAD divisions build upon a common base of three combat brigades of varying strengths and compositions depending on the type and number of battalions used. ROAD divisions are classified according to their special capabilities as either infantry, mechanized, airborne, or armored. A relatively new air assault division emphasizing helicopter-borne infantry has been committed to action in South Vietnam recently. Its success adds another category to this classification of divisions.

59. Jack Raymond, "McNamara Seeks to End Reserve, Enlarge Guard," *New York Times,* December 13, 1964, pp. 1, 84. See also

"Outline of Reserve Realignment," *Army,* XV (January, 1965), 14, 16, 20, and 60.

60. Samuel P. Huntington, "Men at Arms?", *Columbia University Forum,* II (Spring, 1959), 47. Included in this group would be Morris Janowitz, Charles Hitch, Gene Lyons, and John Masland.

61. William W. Kaufmann, *The McNamara Strategy* (New York: Harper & Row, 1964), pp. 80–81.

62. James L. McConaughy, Jr., "Effectiveness of Congress in Military Affairs: How Good Is the Record?", *Fortune,* LVII (April, 1958), 160.

6

OFFICER COLLEGE TRAINING
ROTC Vitalization Act of 1964

6

OFFICER COLLEGE TRAINING
ROTC Vitalization Act of 1964

FOR YEARS, the largest single source of new officers for both active and reserve forces has been the college, or Senior, Reserve Officers Training Corps program known as ROTC. Although the training and recruitment of officers on campus was generally considered successful, the arrangement was regarded primarily as a *reserve* program. Drawing upon the experience gained during fifty years of ROTC operations, Congress in 1964 revised the Reserve Officers Training Corps program.[1] The changes reflected attempts to place greater emphasis on preparation of college men for a professional military career and were foreshadowed by Congressional debate over ten years earlier.[2]

This statutory revision of the ROTC program provides another opportunity to look at the legislative policy-making process for reserve components. A close examination of the process through which the college ROTC program was revised will offer contrasts with other legislative policies adopted for the reserve forces and will assist in gaining a better perspective on the development of a national armed forces reserve. Action in this area of reserve affairs affected the stability of the reserves, the relationship between the executive branch and Congress, and the influence of the Reserve Officers Association.

ORIGIN AND DEVELOPMENT OF ROTC

Authority for the operation of Army ROTC programs was granted in the National Defense Act of 1916.[3] Earlier the Morrill Act of 1862 had required land-grant colleges and universities to offer a course in military training.[4] When the War Department contracts were negotiated with those same institutions in 1916 a compulsory two-year basic course was specified.[5] During the 1920's and the 1930's, the ultimate military objective of the ROTC was the production of reserve officers who were then placed on an inactive status to be called to active duty for two-week training periods, or in time of mobilization.[6] In this period it was difficult to maintain much legislative support for graduates of ROTC programs. Very few of those who wanted to attend two-week training camps to maintain their military skills could get the limited spaces allotted because of budgetary limitations.

Since World War II there has been a gradual increase in the emphasis placed on efforts to encourage ROTC students to consider military life seriously as a professional career.[7] Although the majority still chose a civilian career after a tour of active duty, there was a continuing, but not adequate, source of junior officers for the regular forces. By 1957 there was a growing trend of preparing ROTC graduates for a regular military career, but the primary function of producing reserve officers remained.[8] At that time a change in American military policy was taking place.

There was a transition from a mobilization strategy to a deterrent strategy. This tended to increase the emphasis on both active forces in being and highly ready reserve components as it reduced the emphasis on a large reserve force, much of which needed additional training after an emergency occurred. While the debate raged about the number of reserve forces personnel needed to maintain national security adequately, there was little disagreement about the need for trained professionals in the active forces, preferably with a long-term commitment of service.[9] Given fast-breaking crises in the context of world-wide commitments, it was argued that greater readiness to respond was required of both active forces and the reserve components. It was contended that a large mobilization base of reserve personnel would be false security.

The need for career officers focused on quality as well as quantity. In a period of rapid technological change in military equipment and operational technique, the services were competing with civilian enterprises for the talented personnel required. In recent years the Air Force, more than the other services, has felt that it has not been meeting the competition successfully. There also was a need for officers in the reserve components, especially at the company grade level, and within the civilian components that need was most acute in the Army. Even the National Guard, which has its own officer candidate schools, was trying to sign up ROTC graduates who had fulfilled their active duty obligations.[10] Since the Army required a minimum of two years of active duty from all ROTC graduates, reserve component units could not tap college ROTC sources directly but had to wait until their return to the Ready Reserve.

The development of the ROTC program has also been affected by campus evaluation of military training in a civilian academic setting. There was the juxtaposition of the authority and discipline of military training with the spirit of free inquiry encouraged in academic subjects. Colleges and universities felt obligated to offer the ROTC program as preparation for the responsibilities of citizenship. Most land-grant institutions have made it compulsory for the first two years of college, but this practice is declining.[11] College planning, however, is still cognizant of the practical reality that the ROTC provided a somewhat stabilized student body to insure revenue during periods of national emergency in the past.[12]

In recent years a number of studies and conferences have called for legislative changes in the ROTC program to meet the realities of preparing its graduates for active duty as reservists or regular career officers. One study in 1957 considered the broad goal of the preparation of officers for participation in the formulation of national policies. Its conclusion was that greater use should be made of the nation's colleges and universities to encourage college students to prepare for military careers through the ROTC. Recommendations for accomplishing this goal included the extension of financial assistance to Army and Air Force students similar to that given to the Regular Naval ROTC students.[13]

Another study in 1959, which concentrated on the ROTC, held that programs originally designed for the preparation of reserve officers available in an emergency had come to be used as a source of temporary active duty and permanent career officers. To sustain this new orientation of the ROTC program, it was suggested that a broad scholarship system be instituted, that staff functions in each service for the direction of ROTC programs be lodged in an office dealing with all officer personnel recruitment, not just reserve officers, and that the Reserve Forces Policy Board should coordinate to a far greater degree the ROTC programs of the three services.[14] A national conference at Ohio State University generally confirmed these recommendations and proposed greater flexibility in the program by accepting all qualified junior college graduates transferring to a four-year college for the junior year.[15]

The effort to translate these recommendations into legislative proposals was made in 1961 and 1962 by both the Army and the Air Force at the request of the Department of Defense. At the latter level, as a part of the regular review of all proposals, an advisory panel of prominent educators, established under the Reserve Forces Policy Board considered these and other matters. The panel then developed a number of recommendations, which were in turn adopted as the position of the Board for recommendation to the Secretary of Defense.[16] The Department of Defense legislative proposals included permission to conduct programs of less than four years duration, to increase the retainer payment as well as summer training and travel pay, to allow certain increased administrative flexibility in the operation of the programs at college and university levels, and to permit the awarding of two-year scholarships to Army and Air Force students.[17]

CONGRESSIONAL PROPOSALS FOR REVISION

Although the Junior, or high school, ROTC program had not been the subject of any extensive study, it was the Department of Defense proposal in early 1963 to withdraw financial support from that program which brought the entire ROTC program to the immediate attention of Congress. It was this same provision for high school military training units that later held up the entire ROTC bill until the 1964 civil rights bottleneck had been broken. Protests against the reduction or abolition of high school ROTC included those of a former President:

The local ROTC in our high school was one of my early interests and as a commander of various Reserve units, composed of many ROTC graduates, as well as a Senator and Commander-in-Chief, I believe I know the value of a defense dollar in the Military Establishment.

Record me as opposing reduction, but favoring strengthening the ROTC at high school and college levels.[18]

In response to these reactions, bills were introduced by House Armed Services Subcommittee Chairman Edward Hébert and by its ranking minority member, William G. Bray, not just to sustain the Junior ROTC program but to increase it sevenfold.[19] After two days of hearings, the Department of Defense agreed to a continuation of the Junior ROTC in principle. Action was deferred, however, until the Defense Department could complete its study of the Junior ROTC and until the draft of proposals on the college program was ready. Both programs were then to be handled together before the House Armed Services Subcommittee No. 3 headed by Congressman Hébert.[20]

Administration proposals for both Junior and Senior ROTC programs were combined in H.R. 8130, introduced by Mr. Hébert in August, 1963. In the bill were included provisions from the bills on the high school ROTC program brought out earlier in the year by Mr. Hébert and Mr. Bray, recommendations to continue the Junior program from an *ad hoc* committee appointed by the Defense Department, and plans for permanent reorientation of the college program.[21] Chief features of the plan for college units included the following: authority for an optional two-year program, entrance to which would be based in part on completion of a six-week field training course between the sophomore and junior years; scholarships of two years' duration for selected Army, Navy, and Air Force students; permission to increase the retainer pay up to $50.00 per month if the conditions required it; increased travel pay and training pay for field training courses; and greater flexibility in curriculum structure to accommodate local needs as well as those of the separate services.

HOUSE DEBATES EXTENT OF REVISION

From the House hearings in September and October of 1963 came the major conclusion from all participants that the Senior ROTC program had to be revised. It was an economical way to produce officers for the armed services, but there was a desire to attract a greater number of high quality students with the hope that they would select a professional military career. There also was a need to retain the more traditional purpose of the ROTC of providing junior officers for active reserve units. Controversy arose over the extent to which the program should be changed. The Department of Defense, the three military departments, and the colleges and universities strongly supported the administration measure, which called for extensive, permanent departures from the established programs. Senior members of the House Armed Services Subcommittee on Reserve Affairs and the Reserve Officers Association desired to retain as much of the past program as possible and to experiment with a few temporary changes, such as the two-year program and scholarships for those in the four-year program.

The extent and direction of the changes in the Senior ROTC program were evaluated on the basis of the projected need for junior officers in each service and on the basis of other values such as the development of citizenship responsibilities. The over-all mission was to provide qualified officers as required for the active and the reserve forces according to Deputy Secretary of Defense for Manpower and Reserve Norman Paul.[22] Without the ROTC the services would be unable to meet force requirements at the junior officer level in either the regular or the reserve components. The need was for active and reserve force officers, but the Department of Defense placed greater emphasis on the former category.

The Air Force was especially interested in an entirely voluntary two-year program for the junior and senior college years with a scholarship feature to cover tuition, books, and fees. Its old program, which operated under the 1916 National Defense Act before the Air Force was even created, was not sufficiently attractive to make it possible to produce the number of officers needed for the active establishment.[23] Besides quantity, the Air Force needed men of quality, particularly in the fields of science and engineering. It was thought that a two-year scholarship program would broaden the base of selection for higher quality people by including for consideration junior college transferees, engineering and science students with a heavy academic load, and those who might be tempted to prepare themselves for civilian jobs in private industry. Since the Air Force Reserve was not fully manned, it was hoped that the new program for increasing the number of active duty officers would also help the Reserve situation.[24]

The Army was also in need of junior officers. In early 1962 it was falling about 3,000 short in annual output of ROTC graduates for its active and reserve force requirements according to Secretary of the Army Elvis Stahr.[25] The succeeding Secretary of the Army, Stephen Ailes, expected a scholarship program to increase the chances of attracting high-caliber students and to encourage them to consider a professional military career.[26] In fiscal year 1963 the Army obtained its regular officers from West Point and appointments (498), from the ROTC distinguished military graduates (727), and from the integration of active duty officers into a regular status (1,000).[27]

Since the ROTC program was the largest and most important single source of officer personnel for Army reserve components, any abandonment of the program or serious reduction in the number of graduates would seriously jeopardize the ability of the reserves to perform their function during mobilization according to the Deputy Chief of Reserve Components, Brigadier General Thomas A. Kenan.[28] Both the Reserve Officers Association and the National Guard expressed concern about meeting future reserve component requirements.[29] If the over-all Army production remained about the same and a large percentage stayed on for careers, then the reserve components would have less to choose from for its needs. The National Guard had state officer candidate schools, but, both in number and quality of the product, there were growing signs of difficulty in this area.[30]

Navy experience with both its Regular (Holloway) program, in which a student received tuition, fees, and retainer pay for four years and with its contract program, in which the student received retainer pay for the last two years, gave it solid reason to support an extension of a scholarship program for all three departments.[31] In fiscal year 1963 input in the Holloway program increased from 1,685 to 2,281 students because of favorable retention experience and the desire to have officers of high technical competence.[32] In a comparison of Holloway graduates with Naval Academy graduates, only 38 per cent of the Regular ROTC graduates remained on active duty beyond their obligated time, whereas about 85 per cent of the Annapolis graduates remained beyond their obligated time. However, the cost for a Holloway man was only $9,000 compared with a cost of $36,000 for an academy graduate.

Educators strongly approved the approach to officer recruitment proposed by the Department of Defense in a revised Senior ROTC program. John Masland, an authority on ROTC affairs, spoke for the American Council on Education in favor of the principle of greater federal support. This could be done with scholarships for a program whose central function he thought was now acknowledged to be the production of professional officers for the armed forces.[33] He advocated a two-year program as a professional approach to officer training for these reasons: the many demands on a student's time, including extracurricular interests; the costs of the four-year program; and the high rate of attrition between the basic and advanced courses. His only concession to a four-year course was that the basic course offered a two-year screening process for the selection of advanced ROTC students.[34] Masland pointed to the curriculum as the area in which educators had perhaps the most legitimate concern. In this respect his recommendation was for as little instruction as possible on campus of the kind available at military installations or during extensive periods of summer field training or cruises.[35]

The Association of State Universities and Land-Grant Colleges through Dr. O. C. Aderhold, President of the University of Georgia, placed emphasis on the growing pressure for more facilities created by increased enrolments. In addition to the reasons cited by Dr. Masland, Dr. Aderhold indicated that a two-year program would go a long way toward reducing space requirements. It was also suggested that since his group of colleges generally had lower tuitions than private institutions, a fairer system of federal contribution would be the payment of a flat fee to all schools.[36]

As the testimony unfolded it became clear that House Armed Services subcommittee Chairman Edward Hébert had definite ideas about some of the features that should emerge in legislative proposals. Foremost among these were the convictions that the four-year program should be preserved and that any deviation from it would be on a trial basis only. Although the matter of compulsory ROTC training for the first two years of college was left to state and local option, the principle of such training was affected by the choice of the four- or the two-year programs. If the committee made an unqualified endorsement of the two-year program, a large number of schools would probably drop the four-year program. In terms of officer production only, the attrition rate was high in the four-year programs. However, if the values of patriotism, leadership, confidence, and citizenship were accepted as goals along with the production rate, then having as large a segment of college youth exposed to ROTC through a compulsory system was desirable.[37]

Although the services felt that a voluntary program was more desirable, somewhat conflicting evidence existed on officer production figures in voluntary and compulsory situations. At Arizona State University about 60 per cent of the advanced students going on for commissions indicated they would *not* have registered for ROTC had it been elective.[38] The Air Force production percentage for fiscal 1963 was much higher for elective schools than for compulsory ones.[39] Generally, total enrolment dropped off at a college when the compulsory requirement was lifted, but end production was only slightly affected.[40]

Another goal favored by Mr. Hébert was movement toward a more uniform system of ROTC for all services. While he acknowledged that the needs of each service were somewhat different, Congressman Hébert saw the hope of a more uniform system through experimentation with a scholarship plan.[41] The success of the Navy scholarship program (Holloway plan) provided persuasive evidence that the scholarship feature should be included in the program for the Army and the Air Force. Use of scholarships by the Army would probably extend the active-duty tour for its recipients to be more closely in line with the four-year requirement for the Air Force and the four- and three-year requirement for Navy ROTC students.

Strong support for Mr. Hébert's views came from the Reserve Officers Association. It was willing to back any program that would provide the active forces with a stable and highly competent corps of officers as long as it did not ignore or downgrade the development of officers for the reserve forces.[42] It would approve additional emphasis on securing officers for active duty, but it would not support action to deny the original and historic mission of the ROTC to develop military leaders among citizens to serve in national emergencies.

The ROA was particularly interested in preserving a four-year program for the three service ROTC's. For land-grant colleges the ROA urged the retention of compulsory training because it held that the program made a distinct contribution to the development of patriotism in youth. If the Air Force were primarily concerned with innovations in its recruitment efforts, the ROA suggested experimentation with a Holloway-type program, which had clearly proved itself, but it felt the Army program should be left intact.[43] The membership of the ROA was deeply concerned that the introduction of any two-year college plan would erode the four-year program.[44]

Throughout the House hearings on the revision of the ROTC program were numerous illustrations of a Congressional feeling that the executive branch was attempting to undermine legislative authority. Chairman Hébert indicated that whatever plan was adopted, it would not allow any great area of flexibility for the Secretary of Defense to modify the program. Concern over the maintenance of a four-year program led Mr. Hébert to criticize some of the Pentagon personnel as becoming experts the minute they lifted their hands to take the oath of office. In driving for a four-year program and awarding scholarships only to those in the program, Chairman Hébert planned to hold the reins of

Congress so that these features he favored would not lose out to Defense Department proposals.[45]

THE CIVIL RIGHTS AMENDMENT OBSTACLE

The results of the extensive House hearings were incorporated in a revised committee bill, H.R. 9124, brought out on November 14, 1963.[46] The main features that differed from the administration proposals in H.R. 8130 dealt with the eligibility for scholarships, the amount of retainer fee for the advanced phase of the Senior program, and the extent of the expansion of the high school program. Although the bill authorized each service to establish a two-year college program, scholarships were to be awarded only to those in a four-year program for periods of from one to four years. Authority to award the scholarships would be permissive, but in no event could the number exceed ceilings of 8,000 each for the Army, the Navy, and the Air Force. The Department of Defense had sought scholarships for the two-year program. House Armed Services Subcommittee No. 3 recommended mandatory monthly retainer payments of $50.00 for advanced students as contrasted with the Department of Defense request for only permissive authority to raise the amount to $50.00.[47]

Concerning the matter of high school ROTC, there was a difference not only between the committee bill and the department bill but also a difference of opinion within the full House Armed Services Committee. The committee bill provided for an increase to 2,000 participating schools, whereas the Department of Defense had reluctantly pledged eventual extension to 1,200 schools. Within the committee, seven members appended a statement to the committee report and sought an additional requirement for high schools

desiring to establish ROTC units. Besides requiring a minimum number of 100 cadets for each unit and a three-year
military training course, these seven committee members
wanted as a third condition the provision that a high school
could not deny admission to the ROTC program to any student
on the grounds of his race or color.[48] When their amendment
to the bill was tabled by a vote of 17-14 in the House Armed
Services Committee, they pledged to seek adoption of the
change during the floor debate.

Since there was a threat of a civil rights amendment
occurring in the floor debate, Chairman Hébert chose to
call the bill up for action on December 2, 1963, under the
suspension of rules procedure. With this method no amendments could be offered, and debate would be limited to forty
minutes. However, a two-thirds majority vote is required
for passage. Representative Otis Pike led the opposition and
declared that it was unfair that any important bill that fourteen out of thirty-one committee members desired to amend
be put on the calendar under the suspension of rules.[49]
Chairman Hébert's defense was that protection against segregation in the high school ROTC program could be handled
by the executive departments, which he felt would not allow
it. With no opportunity to include a civil rights amendment
in H.R. 9124, the only alternative for those who wanted
an amendment was to vote against the entire bill. Out of the
330 House members voting, only 176 responded in the
affirmative. The bill was thus forty-four votes short of
passage.[50]

During the second session of the Eighty-eighth Congress,
reconsideration of the ROTC bill was postponed until work
on the Civil Rights Act was almost completed. Chairman
Hébert realized that until the type of amendment that
blocked the ROTC bill was included as a provision of the
Civil Rights bill it would not be wise to call up his bill for
another vote. As the time for action grew shorter, many

other bills competed for attention, creating the possibility that the ROTC bill would die. The President of the ROA was pessimistic about the chances of the ROTC bill in the spring of 1964 because of the long wait that was expected on the Civil Rights bill.[51] However, after the Civil Rights measure had passed both houses the first time, those who had insisted on a civil rights amendment for high schools in the ROTC bill no longer felt such a need.[52] Mr. Hébert's personal interest in the bill and the desire of the Department of Defense for immediate revision in the ROTC program also contributed to the revival of H.R. 9124. On June 23 the House passed H.R. 9124 on to the Senate as Chairman of Armed Services Committee Carl Vinson made the last major speech of his career in Congress before retirement in support of the bill.[53]

CHANGES THROUGH SENATE ACTION

At the Senate hearings the Department of Defense continued to work for a two-year program with scholarships. The ceiling under consideration was 8,000 for each service, but the Department planned to use only 1,000 for each service at the beginning.[54] Representatives of major college organizations again supplemented the arguments for a two-year program. They stressed the need for increased federal support financially both to schools and to individuals. Although they recognized a responsibility to contribute to national defense efforts, they also pointed to the ever burgeoning demands of increased enrolments. The Reserve Officers Association maintained its strong position for four-year programs for scholarship and non-scholarship students, in which junior college transferees would be allowed to enter the advanced ROTC in the third year after completing an intensive summer training course of six weeks.[55] Senator

Richard Russell, Chairman of the Senate Armed Services Committee, agreed substantially with the Reserve Officers Association. Veterans' organizations such as the American Legion, the Military Order of the World Wars, and the Veterans of Foreign Wars encouraged retention of existing high school and college ROTC programs without excluding experimentation with a two-year college program. The needs of Army reserve forces also received consideration, but no specific provisions were made for them. A shortage of 5,000 junior officers for the Army National Guard and 5,000 for the Army Reserve was claimed.[56]

The Senate Armed Services Committee report emphasized the two major differences in the attitudes of the Congress and the Department of Defense concerning changes in the ROTC. Under the Department proposal, if a college chose a two-year program, then a four-year program would be ruled out. The committee position would permit both two- and four-year programs to operate simultaneously on the same campus. In reference to scholarships, the Department of Defense position would make two-year program students eligible for financial assistance while the Armed Services Committee would limit eligibility to those in a four-year ROTC program.[57] In each instance the committee views prevailed.

Two major changes were made by the Senate to lower the cost of the bill. The total number of scholarships for each service was reduced from 8,000 to a permissive ceiling of 5,500—only 4,000 of which could be used immediately in the Army and the Air Force programs. Retainer pay for the two years of the advanced courses would be reduced to a mandatory minimum of $40.00 instead of $50.00 but with a permissive maximum of $50.00.[58]

On the floor of the Senate, the only threat to any portion of H.R. 9124 was aimed at the expansion of the high school program. Senator Gaylord Nelson of Wisconsin proposed to limit the Junior ROTC program to 300 schools, or about the number of those already in existence instead of the gradual expansion up to the 1,200 schools contained in the bill. His amendment was defeated decisively, and the measure passed without difficulty on September 28, 1964.[59] Two days later the House concurred in the Senate amendments.[60]

In final form the law made some significant changes in the ROTC program. Preservation and future expansion of the high school program was confirmed. Not more than 200 new units could be established per year by all military departments beginning in 1966. The total number of high school units that could be established and maintained could not exceed 1,200. At the college level, institutions could adopt either a two- or a four-year program or both, but scholarships without specific tuition limits would be available only for selected students in the four-year program for periods of one to four years. Those who accepted scholarships would be obligated to serve four-year tours of active duty. To enter the two-year program, an applicant would have to complete successfully six weeks of field training or a practice cruise. Students in the last two years or advanced course would get a minimum retainer payment of $40.00 per month for a maximum of twenty months.[61] Entitlement to pay for field training or practice cruises was increased to the rate received by cadets and midshipmen of the regular service academies. Curriculum flexibility was established by permitting the Secretary of each military service to prescribe and conduct the courses of military instruction.[62]

IMPLICATIONS FOR ANALYSIS

The ROTC bill provided a clear illustration of the nature and extent of the power held by a Congressional committee or subcommittee chairman in relation to the scope of the legislation under consideration. As Chairman of the House Armed Services Subcommittee No. 3, Mr. Hébert has built a national reputation as the defender of the Reserves and as an ally of the Reserve Officers Association. He was able to insist on the inlcusion of some features in the bill primarily because they were sponsored by him. Yet when an amendment raised a civil rights issue, he was not able to control other opposing interests that widened the scope of the bill. It was not possible to secure approval for the ROTC bill until the Civil Rights Act of 1964 contained assurances that the Junior ROTC would be supported only in desegregrated high schools. Even the great influence of Carl Vinson in his farewell year as Chairman of the House Committee on Armed Services could not get the bill moving as long as the broader civil rights issue was unsettled.

Congressional primacy of interest in reserve affairs was probably not as clearly asserted in this case as it was in the paid-drill strength or the reserve officer promotion issues. One explanation was that the National Guard did not arouse Congress by participating actively in the process. With state officer candidate schools and an opportunity to secure ROTC graduates, the National Guard Association had less need to participate than did the Reserve Officers Association.

In both houses of Congress, the Reserve Officers Association had allies in key positions. Besides Representatives Vinson and Hébert, the ROA could count on Senator Richard Russell as the Chairman of the Armed Services Committee to work for the goals of the ROA on this issue. Primarily the ROA wanted to preserve the four-year college ROTC plan as a source of reserve officers and as a type of citizenship training. Another goal was to interest high school students in military service as reservists. The entire ROTC program also served as an excellent community relations device with a favorable impact on public opinion.

There was no direct conflict between the ROA and other private groups participating in the legislative process. College organizations such as the American Council on Education and the Association of State Universities and Land-Grant Colleges were not regular actors in the military reserve area and consequently were less effective than the ROA in dealing with Congressional committees, but they did lend a prestigious element to the Defense Department's position. Veterans' organizations were not impressive because their testimony at hearings amounted to little more than general endorsement of the ROTC programs without preferences for changes. The committees listened more out of respect for the reputation of the veterans' groups than out of hope of securing well-articulated recommendations. By contrast the ROA did offer complete, informed testimony that was valuable to the committee in reaching decisions.

The success of the ROA in keeping the proposals within the reserve framework is significant. There had been suggestions that ROTC matters should be considered as part of the total personnel procurement system. For legislative action it was kept in the special reserve category where reserve interests could exert greater influence. Within that setting, the attempt was made to place greater emphasis on training professional career officers. Although the ROTC Vitalization Act of 1964 placed heavier emphasis on the production of military officers for professional careers, it is significant that it was still handled as a reserve program. The college sources of reserve officers were preserved, and the high school training program was expanded. For military manpower needs Congress did not make a choice of major reliance on either professional forces or a predominantly citizen-soldier force. In strategic terms this meant that a situation of massive conventional warfare requiring a large mobilization base of reserve officers was not completely ruled out by Congress. Economically, it was probably not possible to support preparations for every degree of military contingency as adequately as might have been desired, but Congress did provide for each contingency to some extent.

As it had operated in the past, the ROTC program sustained the concept of the citizen-soldier. The Defense Department proposal offered a real threat to the continuation of the program for that purpose. The ROA wanted to gain wide acceptance of the idea that military service was one of the obligations of citizenship, and it was the individual's responsibility to develop whatever talents he might possess to the fullest extent for this duty. Provisions of the act retaining the high school ROTC program and confining college scholarships to four-year cadets should then be interpreted as a way of preserving the citizen-solider concept through the legislative process.

Shortly after statutory changes had been made in the ROTC program, the Secretary of Defense proposed a sweeping realignment and reduction of the Army's reserve components. All the forces at work in the reserve area of the legislative arena were rallied to action. We turn to a detailed examination of this proposal in the next chapter.

Footnotes

1. 78 *Stat.* 1063 (1964) known as the ROTC Vitalization Act of 1964.

2. *Congressional Record*, 83d Cong., 1st sess., 1953, p. 10687.

3. 39 *Stat.* 191 (1916). Three hours of training per week were required. Active duty officers up to the rank of colonel could be detailed for such duty. A six-week period of field training was authorized.

4. 12 *Stat.* 503 (1862).

5. Gene M. Lyons and John W. Masland, *Education and Military Leadership* (Princeton: Princeton University Press, 1959), p. 45. This was contested at the University of Wisconsin and the courts ruled

the compulsory feature non-enforceable. States or local institutions could still impose the compulsory feature if they so chose.

6. *Proceedings of the Regional ROTC Conference*, Lehigh University, May 8–9, 1933 (Washington, D.C.: Civilian Military Education Fund, 1933), p. 82.

7. Lyons and Masland, *op. cit.*, p. 95. Also see Samuel P. Huntington, *The Common Defense* (New York: Columbia University Press, 1961), pp. 436–37.

8. John W. Masland and Lawrence I. Radway, *Soldiers and Scholars* (Princeton: Princeton University Press, 1957), p. 250.

9. Morris Janowitz, *The Professional Soldier* (Glencoe, Ill.: Free Press of Glencoe, 1960), p. 422. Congress was fond of the citizen-soldier for perhaps more than military reasons and blocked replacement of him by a system of complete military professionalism. Support was sought for both reserve and professional forces by Congress.

10. Allen R. Scholin, "The Guard Needs ROTC!", *National Guardsman*, XXXIX (April, 1963), 6.

11. David M. Young, "ROTC: Required or Elective?", *Military Review*, XLII (February, 1962), 22. See also *New York Times*, December 19, 1963, p. 30. The University of Illinois was one of the large schools to put ROTC on a voluntary basis for freshmen and sophomores recently.

12. Richard H. Ostheimer, *Student Charges and Financing Higher Education* (New York: Columbia University Press, 1953), pp. 12–25, 35.

13. Masland and Radway, *op. cit.*, p. 267. Virtually an entire college education is underwritten through payments of tuition, fees, books, and $50.00 per month for four years in the Regular Naval ROTC program, also referred to as the Holloway program.

14. Lyons and Masland, *op. cit.*, pp. 239–40. This study to analyze the ROTC in the light of the requirements of the modern day foreshadowed the major thrust of proposals for the 1964 ROTC Vitalization Act. Research for the study included a conference of prominent educators and military men in June, 1958, at Dartmouth College.

15. Mershon National Security Program, *The Role of Colleges and Universities in ROTC Programs*, Ohio State University, June, 1960, pp. 58–60.

16. House Committee on Armed Services, *Military Reserve Posture Hearings*, Committee Paper No. 66, 87th Cong., 2d sess., 1962, pp. 6324–25. The Advisory Panel on ROTC Affairs consisted of eight, educators chaired by George C. S. Benson, President of Claremont Men's College. The actions were also confirmed by Major General Ralph A. Palladino, Military Executive of the Reserve Forces Policy Board, in a Washington interview on March 27, 1964.

17. Department of Defense, *Annual Report for Fiscal Year 1963* (Washington, D.C.: Government Printing Office, 1964), p. 72.

18. House Committee on Armed Services, *Hearings, Reserve Officers' Training Corps Program*, H.R. 4427, H.R. 4444, H.R. 8130, and H.R. 9124, Committee Paper No. 33, 88th Cong., 1st sess., 1963, p. 6487. A letter from Harry S Truman to the Reserve Officers Association was presented in testimony. The high school program was being conducted at 254 schools at a cost of $4.8 million not including the 625 Army personnel assigned to supervise directly the program. Hereinafter cited as House, *Hearings, ROTC*.

19. *Congressional Record*, 88th Cong., 1st sess., March 4, 1963, p. 3428. Congressman Bray introduced H.R. 4427 and Chairman Hébert, H.R. 4444.

20. House, *Hearings, ROTC*, p. 6511. An *ad hoc* committee was to study Junior ROTC. Legislative proposals for the college program were already in process. See note 16, *supra*.

21. *Ibid.*, p. 6518.

22. *Ibid.*, p. 6517. The entire college program involved 339 colleges and universities in 167 of which the basic course of two years was compulsory. Of the 68 land-grant schools, 61 have ROTC programs and in only 17 of these is the program completely elective.

23. *Ibid.*, p. 6851. In fiscal 1963 from an enrolment of 103,000 cadets the Air Force produced 3,400 officers through ROTC. Its ultimate goal is to graduate between 6,000 and 7,000 officers.

24. *Ibid.*, p. 6630, from the testimony of Benjamin Fridge, Special Assistant to the Secretary of the Air Force. Since Air Force graduates had an active-duty obligation of four years, there are only two years of availability for reserve duty if the officer returns to civilian life when the tour is over.

25. *Ibid.*, p. 6697.

26. *Ibid.*, pp. 6578, 6584.

27. U.S., Department of Defense, *Annual Report for Fiscal Year 1963* (Washington, D.C.: Government Printing Office, 1964). p. 133.

28. House, *Hearings, ROTC*, p. 6631.

29. *Ibid.*, p. 6717.

30. Scholin, *op. cit.*, pp. 6–8. In the past some senior Guard officers chose to ignore the ROTC as a source of junior officers because they preferred to develop them from within the ranks of the Guard. However, by the end of 1964 the Guard estimated there would be a shortage of 12,000 officers needed to fill required positions; state Officer Candidate School classes could not be increased indefinitely in size without diluting the quality of the products. Vigorous recruit-

ing of ROTC graduates was advocated because the Army was expected to release about 6,000 ROTC officers from active duty in fiscal 1964 and in succeeding years. The Guard could offer credit for reserve obligations to ROTC graduates working on an advanced degree before going to active duty. It was also possible for advanced ROTC cadets to affiliate with the Army National Guard while in college and come back to that unit after active duty. In fiscal 1960–62 slightly more than one thousand ROTC graduates came off active duty to the Guard.

31. Graduates of the Holloway program received commissions in the Regular Navy and incurred an obligation to serve for at least four years on active duty. Those graduating from the contract program received a reserve commission and had an active duty obligation of three years.

32. Department of Defense, *Annual Report for Fiscal Year 1963* (Washington, D.C.: Government Printing Office, 1964), p. 201.

33. Carlisle P. Runge, "Improving Officer Recruitment on the College Campus," in *The Role of Colleges and Universities in ROTC Programs*, Mershon National Security Program, Ohio State University, 1960, pp. 34–35. Mr. Runge dissents from the Masland thesis and feels the need exists for large reserve forces for land combat and that ROTC should be sold on positive intellectual arguments of public service and citizenship responsibility. Mr. Runge later served as Assistant Secretary of Defense for Manpower during 1961 and 1962.

34. House, *Hearings, ROTC*, p. 6656. The screening argument should be modified by the consideration that the selection process is limited to those volunteering to continue, and this number is often little more than the desirable quota.

35. A joint civilian-military study group at the Ohio State University reviewed the college Army ROTC curriculum and presented recommendations for change to the Department of the Army near the end of 1964. Its findings were published through the Mershon Center for Education in National Security at the Ohio State University in 1965 under the title *A Proposed Senior Division Army ROTC Curriculum*. Many of the features of this proposed curriculum were scheduled to be introduced in the fall of 1966. A similar study was also conducted by a West Point group as noted in *Officer*, XL (November, 1964), 14.

36. House, *Hearings, ROTC*, p. 6666.

37. Opposition was predicted from large, older schools which consider ROTC courses an adjunct to character development training. Congressmen with big colleges in their districts were expected to give close scrutiny to any proposed changes in the current program. Bill Olcheski, "AFROTC Must Modernize to Meet AF Officer Needs," *Air Force Times*, XXIII (May 15, 1963), 16.

38. Warren W. Hanson, "ROTC, A National Asset that Transcends Military Needs," *Army*, XIV (August, 1963), 33–34.

39. House, *Hearings, ROTC*, p. 6613. Seventy-five per cent of the enrolment was in compulsory schools and accounted for 53 per cent of the output while 25 per cent of the enrolment was in elective schools and produced 47 per cent of the total.

40. *Ibid.*, p. 6614. The evidence on the effect of a change from the compulsory to the elective system on end production from Air Force experience is not conclusive. Rutgers became completely elective in 1960. Prior to that time for a two-year period Rutgers produced 85 Air Force officers. Since that time for a two-year period it has produced 100. In similar time periods after going voluntary in the Air Force program, New York University went up from 43 to 45, St. Joseph in Philadelphia went up from 36 to 46, and Cornell went down from 71 to 32.

41. *Ibid.*, p. 6567.

42. *Ibid.*, p. 6717.

43. "ROA's Fight for AFROTC May Result in Scholarship Program for Air Force," *Officer*, XXXIX (November, 1963), 7.

44. Other groups such as the American Legion and the Veterans of Foreign Wars interested in maintaining the four-year program were not as adamant as the ROA because they indicated they would support two-year programs in colleges where such programs were preferred.

45. House, *Hearings, ROTC*, p. 6720.

46. *Congressional Record*, 88th Cong., 1st sess., 1963, p. 21825.

47. House Committee on Armed Services, *Reserve Officers' Training Corps Program*, H. Rept. 925 to accompany H.R. 9124, 88th Cong., 1st sess., 1963, pp. 21–23.

48. *Ibid.*, p. 31. The statement appended to the report was signed by Representatives Philip Philbin, Melvin Price, Jeffrey Cohelan, Otis Pike, Lucien Nedzi, Robert Stafford, and Richard Schweiker.

49. *Congressional Record*, 88th Cong., 1st sess., 1963, p. 2291. Representative Stratton of New York vigorously supported Mr. Pike in the floor debate.

50. *Ibid.*, p. 22994.

51. Interview with Major General James E. Frank, USAR, Newark, N. J., March 31, 1964.

52. 78 *Stat.* 241 (1964) was passed on July 2, 1964. Title VI on non-discrimination in federally assisted programs covered situations that might previously have been in doubt in an ROTC bill without a civil rights amendment.

53. *Congressional Record*, 88th Cong., 2d sess., 1964, pp. 14692–93.

54. Senate Committee on Armed Services, *Hearings, ROTC Vitalization Act of 1964*, H.R. 9124, 88th Cong., 2d sess., 1964, p. 20.

55. *Ibid.*, p. 63.

56. *Ibid.*, pp. 23, 32.

57. Senate Committee on Armed Services, *ROTC Vitalization Act of 1964*, S. Rept. 1514 to accompany H.R. 9124, 88th Cong., 2d sess., 1964, p. 2.

58. *Ibid.*, pp. 2, 13.

59. *Congressional Record*, 88th Cong., 2d sess., 1964, p. 22981.

60. *Ibid.*, p. 22431.

61. 78 *Stat.* 1063 (1964).

62. See note 35 *supra* on how the Army is carrying out this function.

7

ARMY MERGER PROPOSAL
Realignment of Reserve Components

7

ARMY MERGER PROPOSAL
Realignment of Reserve Components

THE MOST RECENT EPISODE in armed forces reserve policy-
making involved the proposal to merge the paid-drill units
of the Army Reserve with those of the National Guard
under the latter's control and to reduce the total number of
paid spaces allotted to the new combination. Officially the
plan was referred to as a realignment of Army reserve
forces. The process through which the proposal passed has
brought into clearer focus the major elements that have
been interacting in reserve policy decisions since the end
of World War II. Not only has the merger proposal provoked
an intense interest within the Armed Services and Appropriations committees of both houses of Congress and
kindled new tension between the executive and legislative
branches of the national government over the constitutional
authority to establish defense forces, but it has also offered
an opportunity to appraise the role of the reserve forces in
our national defense strategy and to measure the adequacy
of the citizen-soldier concept.

The merger issue has also stimulated other related activity that has become enmeshed in the consideration of changes in the Army reserve components. As one of the organizations most directly interested in the merger, the Reserve Officers Association has been prompted to mobilize its entire resources to block the proposal. State governors have become concerned with the reorganization of their major protective force for large-scale emergencies. Loyalties to military units and to each component have risen to inject an emotional tone into the policy determination process.

Two basic issues are involved in the merger proposal. One deals with the authority to determine how the reserve components of the armed forces will be organized to meet the military requirements of national strategy—How far can the Secretary of Defense go without Congressional approval? The second relates to the substance of the reorganization plan itself—What features should be incorporated into the structure of the Army reserve components? Without assigning as high a priority to the merger proposal as to nuclear weapons development and control or to the commitment of American forces in Vietnam, it is worthwhile to analyze the merger issue as an instructive example of the role of Congress in the formulation of national security policy.

THE 1965 RESERVE ENVIRONMENT

As its eighty-ninth term dawned, Congress continued to find itself playing a declining role in national defense policy–making. The initiative had long since passed to an expanding executive bureaucracy. One change in the House Armed Services Committee offered promise of a renewed challenge to executive influence, however. When Representative L. Mendel Rivers became chairman of that committee, the curtain came down on the Carl Vinson era. Almost immediately Chairman Rivers announced his intent to restore the integrity of Congressional authority to raise and support armies and navies as well as other associated powers. Although Vinson had been the undisputed Congressional champion of the armed services, it is also true that he usually found himself accommodated to Pentagon desires. There was promise too that Congress would continue to maintain its abiding interest in the reserve components of the armed services by carefully examining any proposals to alter their structure or strength.

The Secretary of Defense continued to enjoy the full support of the President, now sustained in his own right by an impressive national vote. While burdened with the greater demands of American military involvement in Vietnam, Secretary McNamara proposed a reorganization of the Army reserve components that would place the active reserve units completely under National Guard control. Since his assumption of office in the Kennedy administration, the Secretary had made rigorous use of the powers granted to him under the Reorganization Act of 1958 in consolidating activities in the Defense Department. He dazzled congressmen with his documentation of defense needs and in some cases irritated their sensitivities as he implemented his programs. Along the way professional military men were brought under strong civilian control, and their day of overturning Defense Department proposals by gaining sympathetic Congressional support had passed. One goal with which Congress could not quarrel was the McNamara insistence on securing the defense capability needed at the lowest possible cost.

Gradually a defense strategy evolved that ruled out any plan for a mobilization of reserve forces on the scale of World War II. The validity of the citizen-soldier concept was still acknowledged, but its importance was scaled down, whereas the degree of readiness was to be improved within reserve units. Army plans began to embrace a twenty-two to twenty-four division deployable force with six to eight of those divisions coming from the reserve components. At the same time America's commitment to South Vietnam demanded more active forces in Southeast Asia, and this thinned the ranks of the continental strategic reserve. Any reserve reorganization plan, whatever its merits, evoked an almost reflex-type opposition from armed services specialists in Congress when it included a reduction in the strength of the reserve components of the Army, as this reorganization plan did. This opposition grew with the possibility of a callup of reserve forces because it was difficult to envision a reorganization's being conducted in the midst of a callup.

Since World War II the National Guard and the Reserve of the Army have been allowed to develop in somewhat parallel fashion with the edge in financial assistance given to the National Guard. At one point early in the postwar period, the Gray Committee on Civilian Components did propose a merger of the two Army reserve components under complete federal control, but this recommendation was not accepted.[1] The National Guard tended to concentrate on combat units while the Reserve added combat units to its logistical support and training units, although its greatest strength still resided in its combat support and training capabilities. Both state and federal missions were assigned the National Guard force while the Army Reserve had only a federal mission.

For the past decade authorized and programmed strength levels for the two Army reserve components have remained steady, but the actual strength has fluctuated for a number of reasons. The number of recruits rapidly increased after the passage of the Reserve Forces Act of 1955, but then efforts were made to keep the number down during the last few years of the Eisenhower administration. The Berlin recall also reduced the actual strength levels of both components, and various Department of Defense measures have generally kept actual strength below the authorized levels. Just prior to the announcement of the merger proposal in December, 1964, the combined actual strength of the two Army reserve components was approximately 60,000 below the authorized paid-drill level of 700,000.[2] It would probably be fair to say that the authorized paid-drill levels were goals that the two components and their backers hoped to reach, but they were not necessarily figures related to military requirements based on contingency war plans.

During the postwar period a rivalry has grown up between the two reserve components of the Army, and organized groups have sought to protect the interests of each. Neither component relished any confrontation with the other, and as long as each got what it thought it should have in the way of funds to develop its forces a "live and let live" feeling evolved. Both the National Guard Association and the Reserve Officers Association found strong backing in Congress, and, prior to the merger proposal, any executive-initiated reduction in reserve component strength had not shown preference for either group over the other. This was true of the attempted budget reduction in 1958-60 and in the reorganization plan of 1962 in which each component lost four combat divisions. In the past two years the leadership of the National Guard Association has changed and with it has come an attitude of trying to work more closely with the Pentagon. Among other reasons this no doubt affected the Army appraisal of a single management system of the reserve components lodged under National Guard control.

Another factor in the reserve environment was that many of the World War II veterans who had remained in the reserve components were approaching the point of qualifying for retirement pay through reserve service. There was some fear that reduction in training opportunities for high-ranking officers would make it difficult for them to reach the twenty-year mark of satisfactory service required for retirement benefits. Attention was then drawn to the retirement costs in future years if the reserve program continued on a large scale. It raised the question of the motivation of those vociferously protesting reduction in reserve forces. Were they objecting on grounds that a reduction in paid-drill strength would weaken national security or were they objecting because the opportunity to qualify for personal benefits might be lost?

MERGER ANNOUNCEMENT AND INITIAL REACTIONS

At a news conference on Saturday, December 12, 1964, Secretary of Defense Robert McNamara revealed his intention to reorganize the reserve components of the Army. He proposed a plan in which all paid-drill units would be placed under the single management of the National Guard. Some units of both components for which there was no military requirement in contingency war plans would be discontinued, and the authorized paid-drill strength of the combined components would be reduced from 700,000 to 550,000. With the unit structure of the Guard and the Reserve merged under the management of the National Guard, the Army Reserve would consist entirely of individuals and provide personnel for units at summer camp or upon mobilization.[3]

A number of significant objectives were sought by the Department of Defense through the proposed realignment of Army reserve components. First, the plan was aimed at improving the early deployment capability and combat readiness of the reserve forces. Second, it was designed to bring the reserve component structure into balance with the contingency war plans and the related equipment procurement program. Third, there was the desire to streamline the management structure of the reserve components. Although the merger was not launched with the major concern of reducing defense expenditures, the Secretary of Defense did point to an expected cost savings of approximately $150 million per year.

Two other measures were also disclosed at the same Pentagon news conference. Although these measures were not directly related to the merger plan, they did affect the atmosphere of its reception. Instructions were issued to transfer reservists holding key civilian positions in the three branches of the federal government from the Ready Reserve to the Standby Reserve. Among the 150,000 federal employees in the Ready Reserve, it was estimated that several thousand were in this key category; eighty-three members of Congress were among those in the Ready Reserve of the various reserve components of the armed services. Ordinarily the transfer to Standby status would make it impossible for them to continue to earn promotion and retirement credit. At the same time new restrictions were imposed on overseas travel by members of Congress who used facilities of the military services. Transportation requested by the chairman of a Congressional committee would be unaffected, but travel initiated by the individual services would be carefully co-ordinated to assure that such travel was oriented to the duties and responsibilities that the Department of Defense and Congress shared.

The plan for realignment had been prepared within the Department of the Army and was recommended to Mr. McNamara by Secretary of the Army Stephen Ailes and General Harold K. Johnson, Chief of Staff of the Army. In a memorandum to Army Reserve commanders sent out on the same day as the news conference, Secretary Ailes pointed out the need for change and that the purchase of training and combat equipment for the 150,000 paid reservists in excess to military requirements would add nearly

$10 billion to defense costs. Reservists who wished to continue to participate in a unit were assured that every reasonable opportunity would be afforded them to do so.

Reactions from those in Congress prominent in the armed services field and from the Reserve Officers Association representing the members of the Army Reserve had one major theme. With solemn fervor they claimed that the realignment plan had to be authorized by Congress before it could be put into effect. The impression from Mr. McNamara's news conference was that the merger was somewhat of a *fait accompli* since consultation with several statutory advisory groups and the appropriate committees of Congress was not scheduled until after the announcement of the plan. Senator John Stennis, Chairman of the Preparedness Investigating Subcommittee of the Senate Armed Services Committee, and Representative F. Edward Hébert, Chairman of the House Armed Services Subcommittee on Reserve and National Guard Affairs, both considered the action of the Defense Department to be a demonstration bordering on contempt of Congress; they expected full hearings prior to implementation of any such plan.[4] The Reserve Officers Association (ROA) in a telegram to the President called the plan a shattering proposal that should be thoroughly analyzed in public hearings before any further action was taken on it by the Department of Defense.[5] In response the President publicly endorsed the McNamara decision as being both prudent and wise.[6] National Guard leaders indicated they were ready to go along with the changes if such action were requested.[7]

THE GATHERING POLITICAL STORM

Newspaper and magazine reports on the merger proposal, in the first few months after its announcement, were generally favorable to its adoption and underestimated the opposition to the plan. The mobilization of resources hopeful of delaying and defeating it was determined but not widespread. Many accounts explained the plan with little analytical comment. There were stories of troop unit allocation for states, of the strength of the McNamara record and his resolve in fighting for a proposal, of the need for streamlining to remove waste, and of changing strategy. Usually the various aspects covered in the articles were developed in a way that drew favorable attention to the plan. Only one nationally prominent critic of the measure pointed out the absence of any adverse analysis as he tried to show why the reform would not work.[8]

The single most active, organized opponent of the plan worked feverishly to stem the tide of change. The Reserve Officers Association encouraged its membership and friends to express opposition to the proposal to both government officials and the general public. Although the ROA pronouncements did contain rebuttals on the merits of the plan, the stress in its releases was on the need for Congressional hearings and the alleged attempt to force a plan through without proper staffing in the defense establishment. Intitially most of this activity occurred at the national level, but it was gradually picked up by local and state levels of the ROA.[9] A major objective was to persuade its membership, other military associations, and a small interested public that the proposal was far from being an accomplished fact.

Within the defense establishment detailed planning for implementation of the proposal moved forward deliberately, if not smoothly. A steering committee was formed within the Office of Reserve Components of the Department of the Army under the direction of its Chief. Representatives of both Reserve and National Guard offices were asked to formulate troop lists and other details involved in the transition. Meanwhile both statutory advisory bodies gave the plan careful consideration. At the Defense Department level, the Reserve Forces Policy Board voted 6-6 on a motion to approve the merger. Within the Department of the Army, the General Staff Committee on National Guard and Reserve Affairs approved the manner of implementing the plan with the Army Reserve members dissenting. Troop lists were sent to the governor of each state to determine whether the proposed realigned force met state requirements for emergency forces.[10]

The actions of the news media, interest groups, and defense-planners produced an understandable anxiety within the paid-drill units of both components. Performance in training sessions was affected by the concern of reservists about drill pay, retirement qualification, transfer to the Guard, fulfilment of obligated service, opportunities for promotion, and discontinuation of units in both components. Strong loyalties to units and components stirred up emotional comments, which added to the turmoil. Although seasoned members of the Army's reserve components can become inured to proposals of this type and continue to perform well despite uncertainty, some dampening of the morale was reflected in training sessions. Morale suffered either from disappointment or disagreement with the estimate of need for less reserve strength manifest in the Defense Department's merger proposal.

Perhaps the most significant element in the gathering political storm over the merger issue was the attitude of the Eighty-ninth Congress on defense matters. Veteran lawmakers in the armed services area sensed the challenge to Congressional authority. The new chairman of the House Armed Services Committee, L. Mendel Rivers, may have felt it necessary when he first assumed his new position to assert his philosophy that he intended to see Congress fulfil its constitutional role in the determination of policy for the armed forces, including the reserve components. He assumed that the merger plan required Congressional approval in principle even before appropriations were considered, and proceeded to organize hearings to get an evaluation of the plan. Beyond resentment of the McNamara approach, it is difficult to determine what other factors may have motivated Congress to take a hard look at the merger proposal.[11] The reserve components were promised their day in court before committees of both houses of the national legislature.

HEARINGS ON THREE FRONTS

The first phase of legislative examination of the merger proposal was conducted by three Congressional groups. Subcommittees of the House and Senate Armed Services Committees delved deeply into how the realignment plan originated as well as its substance after the full Armed Services Committee of the House had made preliminary inquiries. However, before each group the initial and the major emphasis in the consideration of the merger was on the procedure by which the Department of Defense had developed the proposal for reorganization of the Army's reserve components. In this first phase of official legislative review, no request for statutory authority accompanied the merger proposal.

In the House military posture hearings came a revealing preview of the nature of the confrontation between the executive and legislative branches on the merger issue. Mr. Hébert sought a freeze on further Defense Department action until the matter could be fully explored before his subcommittee. Secretary McNamara refused to suspend further preparation of the proposal because he felt it was a necessary part of formulating a complete plan for the Hébert Subcommittee in the House and the Stennis Subcommittee in the Senate. Beyond the need for specific appropriations for an enlarged National Guard force, the Secretary would not concede the need for any statutory permission from Congress to implement the plan. He pledged complete co-operation in fulfilling the intent of Congress on reserve strength levels, even if he were to disagree with the legislative decision. Mr. Hébert made it clear that he personally felt the intent of the laws regulating the reserves had been violated by the Secretary; he vowed that his subcommittee would challenge the Secretary's actions and would require that constitutional provisions for Congressional approval of such a proposal be fully satisfied before any such reorganization of the reserve components took place.[12]

Hearings before the Armed Services subcommittees of both houses were conducted during March and April of 1965. In both situations, as the atmosphere of inquiry was focused on whether the defense establishment was proceeding illegally as it sought to reorganize the reserve components of the Army, the end result was an acknowledgment by the Secretary of Defense that specific legislative provisions would be sought to fully implement the plan.

The legal points in question involved the appropriate use of two advisory groups in the reserve policy area, the transfer of all units out of the Army Reserve, and the use of Reserve personnel in the National Guard on an attached basis. Within the Department of the Army, the General Staff Committees on National Guard and Reserve Policy, which usually met quarterly in joint session, could point to statutory guidance that each policy or regulation affecting such matters as reorganization of the reserve components "shall be prepared" by them.[13] The merger proposal had not been referred to them until after Secretary McNamara had publicly announced that he had instructed the Secretary of the Army to prepare plans to realign the Army's reserve component structure on the basis of a merger into the National Guard. Defense officials claimed the merger was only a concept to be developed, but opponents of the proposal considered it a decision about to be implemented. At the Defense Department level the Reserve Forces Policy Board fulfilled a function somewhat similar to the Army advisory committees. This group also officially received the merger proposal *after* the public announcement of the merger had been made. From the point of view of staffing within the Pentagon, the concept of the merger was handled by a special committee of three officers and reached a comparatively advanced stage of deliberation before it was brought to the attention of the Chief of the Army Reserve.[14] Objections to the plan would undoubtedly have been offered prior to the public announcement if these groups had been called in earlier. Yet Department of Defense witnesses claimed no intent to exclude these groups from final consideration of the plan.

Provisions of the statutes on Army Reserve units and the training of Reserve personnel with National Guard units were also carefully examined. Proponents and opponents of the merger proposal found evidence in the laws to support contradictory interpretations.[15] The heart of the merger plan depended on the authority to remove the unit structure from the Army Reserve. It also became clear that maintenance of the proposed National Guard strength levels during the transition period required more Reservists than were apparently willing to transfer to the Guard voluntarily. The use of Reserve personnel in National Guard training on a temporary basis was to be handled by the administrative procedure of attaching them involuntarily to Guard units if they still had an obligated period of service.

The objectives of the merger proposal were also debated in the hearings, but they never became the central issues. Combat readiness, single management, and military requirements were displaced primarily by an executive-legislative conflict over authority to effect reserve reorganization. The turbulence in the reserve components slowing progress toward training objectives, the process of appointing officers in the National Guard, and the centralization of power in the Pentagon also competed for attention. Both subcommittees expressed disappointment in their attempts to get information. Senate investigators got rather meager returns to requests for information from National Guard officials of the states while the House subcommittee put one Army general under oath to relieve him of whatever qualms he might have about violating institutional restraints on forthright testimony.

The end of the first phase of Congressional inquiry in May, 1965, was marked by a joint news conference by Secretary McNamara and Representative Hébert. The Secretary announced that he would submit a legislative proposal to assure proper legal authority for certain features of the merger. Mr. Hébert was hopeful that Congress had reached full partnership with the defense establishment in the merger deliberations and that the committee's attention could now be focused exclusively on the merits of the plan.[16]

DEATH OF THE MERGER

As a Congressional decision on the merger was delayed, the momentum of the opposition increased. One of the factors that called attention to the significance of reserve components was the decision to commit a larger segment of regular forces to South Vietnam in July, 1965. This decision then made clear the consequent need replenish the continental reserve of the active forces. Although the President chose to use an increased draft rather than a callup of reserve forces to bolster manpower levels, the very fact that a callup of reserve forces had been under consideration was instrumental in convincing many legislators to hold up on approval for a reorganization or a reduction in the strength levels of the reserve components of the Army.[17]

The legislative package promised by the Secretary of Defense met most of the legal difficulties highlighted in the hearings.[18] One provision would have permitted the use of reservists for training and federal missions attached to National Guard units on an involuntary basis. Another section would have authorized the use of reserve personnel of the Women's Army Corps with National Guard units. As a counterproposal to transferring units out of the Army Reserve, Representative Charles Bennett introduced a bill for the retention of units in the Army Reserve, which spelled out the minimum number of paid drills and active duty days on annual field training each year.[19]

As the Hébert Subcommittee reopened its hearings in August, the Defense Department made its final arguments for approval of the merger proposal. Deputy Secretary of Defense Cyrus Vance emphasized the training opportunities that would be made available for those who did not make the change to the Guard. Although such training sessions would be conducted on a non-pay status, they would afford opportunities for reservists to continue earning credit for promotion and retirement purposes while keeping their military skills current.[20]

The decision of the Hébert Subcommittee to conclude its hearings signaled the end for the merger for 1965. Its statement on August 12 indicated that the merger was not in the national interest because it would result in an immediate and serious loss in reserve component capability. The statement also emphasized the subcommittee's determination to resolve the question of future reorganization of the reserve components by recommending positive legislation in the matter.[21] One of the nine subcommittee members, Representative Lucien Nedzi, dissented from the statement and concluded from the hearings that the merger should be put into effect immediately.

The intent of Congress was then reinforced by its action on the Defense Appropriations Act for the fiscal year 1966. Funds were approved for both the Army Reserve and the National Guard with the proviso that the Reserve would be programmed to attain an end strength of 270,000 and the Guard an end strength of not less than 380,000. It was further specified that only upon approval by Congress, through authorizing legislation, of a realignment or reorganization of the Army reserve components could the Secretary of Defense transfer any balance of funds for the support of merged Army Reserve units.[22]

Little time was lost by the Defense Department in reacting to this Congressional guidance. One day after the Appropriations Act had been approved, the Secretary of Defense announced his intention to form a select force of both National Guard and Reserve units and to dissolve 751 Army Reserve units in a paid-drill status with a strength of 55,000 personnel. Representative Hébert conceded that defense officials were within their statutory powers in directing the changes, but Senator Stennis interpreted the action as a violation of the Congressional mandate for delay of any reorganization. Although the Senate Armed Services Committee forwarded a request to the Secretary of Defense to delay the deactivation of the 751 Army Reserve units declared in excess of military requirements by the Defense Department, the Secretary announced his decision to carry out the deactivation plan. Legislation on the reorganization of the Army reserve components then loomed as one of the major items of business for the Armed

Services Committees in the second session of the Eighty-ninth Congress.

CONGRESSIONAL PRIMACY OF INTEREST

In a period when the locus of power in national security policy-making has shifted more decidedly in the direction of the executive branch of government, Congressional insistence on serving as the final authority on changes in the reserve components of the Army is exceptional. The proposal of the executive branch to realign the force structure and reduce the combined strength levels of the Army Reserve and the National Guard has brought the Secretary of Defense into sharp conflict with Congressional leaders in the field of military affairs. The action of Congress in the merger controversy is further evidence of its assertion of a primacy of interest in reserve forces policy-making. The sharpness of the conflict in this situation has arisen because the Department of Defense and Congress have chosen to push their authority to the limit. It is possible to account for the intensity of activity on this issue in part by the nature of the problem and in part by the approach of the individuals playing leading roles.

In the national security area, action on the merger proposal is appealing from the Congressional standpoint of asserting influence because it combines a variety of favorable factors. Organization of the reserve components and establishment of strength levels are problems that can be made explicit in lay terms. No complicated technical data have to be interpreted to analyze the problem. For many congressmen years of association with the reserve components or with active forces during war and national emergencies have given them a first-hand knowledge that is difficult to refute. It could be expected that Congress might react to a reduction in reserve activity in the same way it has reacted to the announcements of the closing of the military bases throughout the country. However, the relatively small group of reservists affected in any one Congressional district does not stir up as great a degree of protest among the general public. To the extent that action in the reserve area arouses a smaller public, congressmen are less restricted in exercising independent judgment in these matters. Individual reservists do not hesitate to communicate their views to congressmen, but the opinions of the reserve component personnel are frequently articulated by strong military associations, such as the Reserve Officers Association and the National Guard Association. In addition, there were specific provisions in the law regarding procedure for developing reorganization plans dealing with reserve components that could be thoroughly investigated in hearings. Finally, there was a growing need for military manpower caused by an expanding United States commitment in South Vietnam.

The personalities and role expectations of governmental leaders also sharpened the conflict in the merger controversy. Despite his great display of talent as an administrator, Secretary of Defense McNamara lacked the tactful attitude required to placate Congressional sensitivities and to perceive the element of compromise in legislative endeavors. Whether justly deserved or not, Mr. McNamara has been characterized by his Congressional adversaries as arrogant. Some of the faith in the McNamara ability was also shaken when estimates on savings and personnel behavior failed to withstand careful Congressional questioning. Where the reorganization procedure was on weak legal footing, the Secretary chose to test rather than consult Congress. In previous years these differences between the Secretary of Defense and Congress might have been adjusted without any major clash, but the new chairman of the House Armed Services Committee, Mendel Rivers, pledged himself to preserve the constitutional power assigned to Congress of regulating the armed forces. Perhaps it was to be expected that in his first year of leadership Mr. Rivers would dramatize his opposition to any undermining of Congressional authority. Senior members of House Armed Services Subcommittee No. 3, which dealt with reserve affairs, were determined to back the chairman in his philosophy of Congressional authority in the merger issue.

The evidence from the legislative action on the merger proposal suggests that Congress has gone beyond its role of what some appraisals have referred to as a monitor of national security policy-making. The Armed Services committees have been stirred to the point of initiating their own legislation to overhaul the Army reserve components— legislation that will undoubtedly seek to define and curb the authority of the executive branch in organizing the reserve force structure and its operations.[23] The previous record of legislative activity in reserve affairs also foreshadows widespread bipartisan support for such a Congressionally-initiated bill.

EFFECTIVENESS OF THE ROA

There was only one major interest group in active opposition to the merger proposal. In over forty years of operation the Reserve Officers Association had not faced a more serious challenge. Representing all federal reserve components, the ROA had special concern for the Army Reserve, since about 60 per cent of its 60,000 members were in that component.[24] The ROA has chosen to interpret its purpose stated in its charter from Congress, "to support a military policy for the United States that will provide adequate national security," to mean for the most part the development of a large military reserve.[25] From the ROA viewpoint the merger proposal could be seen as a threat both to the retention of a major share of its membership and to its basic purpose. Throughout its history the ROA has sought to incorporate detailed provisions in the law for the establishment and operation of the reserve forces so that few actions would be left to administrative discretion. There is hope in the ROA that this goal might prevail in the merger controversy.

The most potent resource of the ROA has been its continuous liaison with Congressional leaders in military affairs and with Congressional reservists, about one hundred of whom can be counted in the Association membership list. Used somewhat like a specialized intelligence network, the ROA has been able to supply a rather substantial amount of information for Congressional deliberations. For its contributions the ROA could usually depend on a sympathetic ear. At the same time, no doubt, the national reputation of Congressional leaders in military affairs has also been fostered by help from the Reserve Officers Association. Of great value to Congressional consideration of reserve affairs has been the facility of the ROA to spell out in personal terms the implications of various policy proposals.

In its work the ROA has offered strong direction from the national level and has been able to move back and forth across the line between civilian and military with great agility. The permanent staff in Washington is comprised of an experienced and competent group of retired military officers with strong ties in policy-making areas. They have been able to alert the elected officers and the general membership to the tides of reserve affairs. State and local organizations forge the link with influential groups and their governmental representatives. Reservists, essentially civilians, have been able to function politically as citizens in matters of military policy where professional military people would be restrained. Probably in the hopes of promoting organization cohesion and stimulating members to action, association information releases have occasionally indulged in personal attacks as well as significant exaggerations and omissions.

The ROA influence in the White House and the Pentagon have declined since the days of the Truman administration, but there are still strong points throughout the executive branch. President Truman regarded himself as one of the charter members of the ROA and could usually be relied upon to support the programs of the reserve components. In the McNamara tenure the ROA has had to rely on its rapport with the separate services to counter the coolness at the Defense Department level. There has been a noticeable ROA concern about the ability of the rival National Guard Association to establish what appears to be an effective working relationship with the Pentagon at both service and Department of Defense levels.

Should the apparent success of the ROA in the merger issue be any cause for alarm in the national security policy-making area? Insofar as the legislative aspects of military policy-making are concerned there seems to be little basis for any fear that domestic pressures generated by the ROA outweigh an evaluation of strategic considerations in reserve affairs. Although the ROA can mobilize significant opposition, it has far from enough influence to determine the direction of policy. The ROA is highly regarded in its field of interest but certainly not deserving of any estimate of its influence suggesting it could exert enough pressure to overwhelm national legislators on any issue it chose.

CIVILIAN CONTROL

Action on the merger proposal illustrates how the separation of powers in the national government and the political involvement of members of the Army reserve components in the policy-making process affect the civilian control of the military. Using the guidelines of Samuel Huntington's analysis of civilian control, one would have to conclude that the fragmentation of authority over the military, originally designed by the Framers of the Constitution to keep any group from gaining complete control of the military, has permitted semimilitary forces as embodied in the reserve components to assert effective political leverage in decisions on force structure and strength levels.[26] Although this has hampered civilian control, it has certainly not endangered the acceptance of civilian control by the professional military people.

The problem has stemmed from the fact that reservists play dual roles as citizens and soldiers. In the McNamara period reservists have found it more difficult to enlist the support of professional military men in their interests because the Secretary of Defense has exercised a tight rein over the three services. Parenthetically, it should be indicated that in the past the process of reservists' getting professional military support had been part of a two-way street on which professional military people in return sought the help of reservists in gaining features for programs for the active forces. During the attempt to reduce the paid-drill strength of the Army reserve components in the last few years of the Eisenhower administration, the defense establishment was a house divided facing a united military reserve seeking to block the reduction. Even though the attempt at reduction of reserve forces failed then and the attempt to merge failed in 1965, it was a much closer contest in the latter case.

As the influence of the professional military has declined and as the success of military associations in drawing them into the political arena has diminished, the personnel of the reserve components have been forced to intensify their efforts to maintain their strength levels. In particular, the Reserve Officers Association has found it necessary to mobilize its every resource, especially since the choice of the Guard as the manager of the proposed merged force effectively removed the National Guard Association from any opposition to the Defense Department plan. Thus, as the professional military have become less politically involved in military manpower decisions, reservists have stepped up their political action in the policy-making process by pressing legislators to support the Army Reserve in the struggle to preserve the unit structure in that component.

In its bid to participate more fully in national security policy decisions, Congress is at some disadvantage in comparison with the executive branch. Congressmen have been concerned about the restraint under which professional military leaders express evaluations of defense proposals. In public hearings and in private interviews, legislators said they often found it difficult to separate the personal opinions of the military from the policy guidance established by the Department of Defense.[27] Part of this frustration may arise from the lawmaker's attempt to find justification in professional advice for an already firmly-drawn conviction. Several of the unsettled questions in the merger hearings involved the extent to which the professional military was responsible for the conception of the merger proposal and the degree of enthusiasm with which it subscribed to the plan. Only one high-ranking staff officer, the Chief of the Army Reserve, who by common practice is a reservist on extended active duty for a special tour in the Pentagon, opposed the merger plan when it was examined by Congress. His position might have been expected to favor the Army Reserve; with this exception all professional military men supported the plan for merger.

THE MODERN CITIZEN-SOLDIER

Through all the deliberations on the merger proposal, one thread of agreement emerged. The concept of the citizen-soldier was still valid in national security planning. However, the modern version of the citizen-soldier embodied a greater capability and degree of readiness than any of the earlier editions did. Grounded on economic necessity and the need for military strength to match world-wide commitments, the concept of the American citizen-soldier provided an added bonus for the defense establishment as an information channel to communities throughout the country.

Ideally, civilian and military leaders would prefer to have their military capability exclusively in the active forces. The economic consequences of such a choice could be met but at the expense of other sectors of the economy. Since World War II the military requirements of the United States for trained manpower to fulfil contingency war plans have been on a higher level than what the active forces have been able to meet. The proportion of active forces and reserve components in the total manpower picture has varied, but there has always been the need for a mix of the two.

The modern citizen-soldier slated for early callup in contingency planning will spend considerably more of his time than in the past to attain the desired capability and state of readiness. In fact, there has been some concern that the quality of the individual able to devote the time required for reserve training might be somewhat lower than the caliber of personnel now involved. In the new Select Reserve Force of 150,000 from the two Army reserve components, training time alone will consume a minimum of eighteen full weekends. There is a good chance that the annual two-week period of field training will be extended. Staff planning and administrative work will undoubtedly require some additional time beyond the above allotment for part of the force. Will personnel be able to carry on civilian pursuits under such conditions, and will employers be interested in personnel who must restrict their regular civilian work or, at the least, have less time to rest from their civilian labors?

A stepped-up screening process is already removing top federal employees from active reserve participation with Ready Reserve units. Of course, there is no quarrel with not giving a man reserve training if his governmental position would not enable him to respond to a callup in a national emergency. Nevertheless, the reserve components are facing the fact that highly qualified reservists might have to decide against reserve participation if they recognize that promotion to a responsible position would probably remove them from reserve activities before they could reach higher rank and qualify for retirement benefits. The extension of this screening process to private enterprise would present promising leaders with the same dilemma faced by government employees.

Military planners also acknowledge the value of the citizen-soldier as a representative of the defense establishment in communities throughout the country. Reserve officers are frequently influential citizens and can help to mold local community attitudes favorable to military activities. Information from the military offices can be effectively disseminated in this way, and an image worthy of respect can be cultivated.

One last consideration about the pressure on the citizen-soldier can probably be dismissed rather quickly, but it has occasionally flitted through the minds of reservists. Is it possible that professional military people support a plan such as the merger proposal because they perceive the citizen-soldier as a threat to guild ethos and are resentful of the benefits accorded the citizen-soldier for his avocational pursuit? In the last two decades the barrier between regular and reservist has almost completely disappeared through more frequent and satisfactory working contact. Indeed, there are some reservists who possess expertise not found in the regular military ranks. It would appear, then, that there is a genuine appreciation in both groups of the value of the other to national security.

Perhaps the over-all effect of this merger issue will be the development of a greater awareness of the role of the citizen-soldier. This will probably bring improvements in the reserve components, though the method of bringing them about will remain in dispute.

As the substantive issues of armed forces reserve problems have been considered, the Reserve Officers Association has frequently appeared as a major participant in the legislative process through which policy has developed. Before reaching final conclusions on this process, it would be profitable to examine the ROA more closely. The next chapter will then be devoted to an analysis of this interest group.

Footnotes

1. *Army and Navy Journal,* LXXXV (August 14, 1948), 1379. This article quotes in detail from *Reserve Forces for National Security,* Report to the Secretary of Defense by the Committee on Civilian Conponents, June 30, 1948, pp. 9–18.

2. Senate Committee on Armed Services, Preparedness Investigating Subcommittee, *Hearings, Proposal to Realine the Army National Guard and the Army Reserve Forces,* 89th Cong., 1st sess., 1965, p. 132.

3. House Committee on Armed Services, Subcommittee No. 2, *Hearings, Merger of the Army Reserve Components*, Committee Paper No. 39, 89th Cong., 1st sess., 1965, pp. 3573–75. Hereinafter cited as House, *Hearings, Merger.*

4. *New York Times*, December 11, 1964, p. 18.

5. *New York Times*, December 13, 1964, p. 1.

6. *Army Times*, December 23, 1964, p. 16.

7. *New York Times*, December 13, 1964, p. 1; *Journal of the Armed Forces*, CII (January 9, 1965), 30–31.

8. S. L. A. Marshall, "McNamara's Latest Reform: Why His National Guard Scheme Won't Work," CLII *New Republic* (January 23, 1965), 13–15.

9. *Officer*, XVI (February, 1965), 8–9, 14.

10. House, *Hearings, Merger*, pp. 3983–84.

11. Interviews with Senator Margaret Chase Smith, Representatives F. Edward Hébert, Lucien Nedzi, Alton Lennon, William G. Bray, Alexander Pirnie, Charles E. Bennett, and Robert L. F. Sikes, and former Secretary of the Army Stephen Ailes in Washington, D. C., October 11–14, 1965.

12. House Committee on Armed Services, *Hearings on Military Posture and H.R. 4016*, Committee Paper No. 7, 89th Cong., 1st sess., 1965, p. 463.

13. 10 *U.S. Code*, 3033.

14. House, *Hearings, Merger*, p. 4057.

15. *Ibid.*, pp. 4320–23.

16. *Ibid.*, Appendix IV, p. xxxiii.

17. *New York Times*, July 29, 1965, p. 1. This reasoning appeared even sounder as two conditions developed in late 1965 and early 1966. First, when 750 Army Reserve units were deactivated, only 1.4 per cent of the personnel voluntarily joined the National Guard. If similar results were to occur under a merger, then there would be a severe loss of manpower. Second, the capability of Army Reserve training divisions, each of which can function as a complete infantry training center, was highlighted when four active Army combat divisions had to be used to provide basic training for the influx of recruits and draftees. These divisions were thus diverted from their primary mission while the Army Reserve training divisions were not used. See Cecil Holland, "Callup of Army Reserves Studied to Meet Shortages," *Washington Star*, April 26, 1966, p. 1.

18. House, *Hearings, Merger,* Appendix III, p. xxxii.

19. *Congressional Record* (Daily Ed.), 89th Cong., 1st sess., 1965, p. 18288. H.R. 10205 was introduced on August 2, 1965.

20. House, *Hearings, Merger,* pp. 4342–43.

21. *Ibid.,* p. 4454.

22. 79 *Stat.* 864, 879 (1965).

23. *St. Louis Post Dispatch,* October 24, 1965, p. 27. This evaluation is based on an estimate given by Representative F. Edward Hébert before the Forty-third Anniversary Banquet of the Reserve Officers Association in St. Louis where Mr. Hébert was honored with the presentation of the association's annual "Minute Man Hall of Fame Award."

24. Interview with Colonel John T. Carlton, Executive Director of the Reserve Officers Association, October 12, 1965.

25. 64 *Stat.* 312 (1950).

26. Samuel P. Huntington, "Civilian Control and the Constitution," *American Political Science Review,* L (September, 1956), 676–99; see also Huntington, "Civilian Control of the Military: A Theoretical Statement," in Heinz Eulau, Samuel J. Eldersveld, and Morris Janowitz (eds.), *Political Behavior: A Reader in Theory and Method* (Glencoe, Ill.: Free Press of Glencoe, 1956), pp. 380–85.

27. See note 11 *supra.*

8

INTEREST GROUP INFLUENCE
Strategy of Reserve Officers Association

8

INTEREST GROUP INFLUENCE
Strategy of Reserve Officers Association

THE RESERVE OFFICERS ASSOCIATION is a potent force, or at least one to be reckoned with, when armed forces reserve policy is considered. Since the end of World War II its involvement in the legislative process has steadily increased in scope, intensity, and effectiveness. In the policies analyzed thus far, with the exception of the force level controversy of 1958–60, the influence of the ROA has been the single determinant outside Congress most responsible for bringing legislative action to a successful conclusion.[1] Congress has become the Association's strongest friend and has provided a secure base for its operations. Within the military departments of the Pentagon, the ROA has established a reputation for competent counsel derived from study and experience.[2] At least one President displayed a high regard and great admiration for the ROA.[3]

For these reasons the background, the internal organization, the setting for action, the mode of operation, and the effectiveness of the Reserve Officers Association will now be examined carefully. Consideration of these aspects of the ROA should contribute to a better understanding of both the policies established and the process through which they became law. An attempt will now be made to assess how the ROA shaped influence in military reserve legislation.

BETWEEN WORLD WARS

The ROA began as a national organization in 1922. In a speech at Washington's New Willard Hotel on October 2 of that year before several hundred officers, many of whom served in the American Expeditionary Force, General John J. Pershing asserted the importance of obtaining continued appropriations for the development of the military reserves.[4] This group of officers was concerned with the role and responsibility of the citizen-soldier, and they agreed fully with General Pershing. Their declared intention was to support and assist in the development and execution of a military policy for the United States that would provide an adequate national defense—a policy in which the citizen-soldier would have an important role. They selected as their first president Brigadier General Henry J. Reilly, General Pershing's confidante who had served under him with an artillery unit.[5]

Throughout the twenties and the thirties the ROA maintained its orientation toward the goal of national preparedness with special emphasis on the training of reserve officers. It worked persistently each year to secure additional funds for active duty training for the reserves.[6] Although the results cannot be attributed directly to such action by the ROA, about 120,000 trained Army Reserve officers were ready to serve at the outbreak of World War II.[7] As a predominantly *Army* reserve officer organization, the ROA gave support to the Citizen Military Training Camps, begun in 1921, and the operation of the Civilian Conservation Corps by reserve officers in 1934.[8] Fighting for greater preparedness also meant a struggle with the pacifist movement.[9] The ROA felt that pacifists would render the United States vulnerable to the expansionist policies of Germany, Japan, and Russia. In these encounters the ROA worked closely with the American Legion under the arrangement of an interlocking directorate.[10] The ROA also assisted the American Legion in its Americanism program. The national ROA level purchased daily data service on Communists and urged 600 chapters to do the same.

During this same period of the twenties and thirties, the ROA was building support for the Reserve among Regular Army leaders. General Douglas MacArthur and succeeding Army Chiefs of Staff, Generals Malin Craig and George C. Marshall, gave public testimonials on the value of a trained reserve component. They had been faced with low levels of preparedness, and the Reserve was welcomed as a partial solution to the problem. General MacArthur often recalled the effective performance of citizen-soldiers during World War I. To focus attention on the value of a trained Reserve as well as on national preparedness, the ROA had established a National Defense Week to be observed annually in the period between the birthdays of Lincoln and Washington. At the invitation of the ROA, General Marshall spoke on a national radio broadcast in 1940 praising the work of the ROA in arousing the nation to the need for military preparedness.[11]

UNIFICATION AND INTERNAL ORGANIZATION

Since World War II the ROA has expanded its activities in scope and refined its techniques of influence. Reactivated by its wartime Board of Trustees in May, 1945, the ROA acquired an executive director, Brigadier General E. A. Evans, who had worked in the War Department on the development of postwar reserve component plans.[12] In 1948 the Reserve Officers of the Naval Services, made up largely of 15,000 World War II reserve officers, merged with the ROA. At about the same time Marine and Coast Guard personnel came into the organization. The creation of a separate department of the Air Force shortly before also brought in that service, and the nation had a reserve association representing all the services for the first time.[13] In 1950 the ROA was successful in its bid for a charter from Congress incorporating the organization with the stated purpose of supporting a military policy for the United States that would provide adequate national security.[14]

Under its constitution the ROA has a representative system of control based on state departments and local chapters. The annual National Convention in June is the highest legislative body. At its sessions national officers are selected for each of the service sections as well as the organization-wide officers.[15] The presidency rotates each year among the three services as the convention usually ratifies the nomination of the service section eligible to hold the office for that year. Deliberations are conducted both in the separate sections for each armed service and in the convention body as a whole. Voting strength by state is based on size of membership.[16]

Second in legislative authority is the National Council, which meets in Washington, D.C., each February. It is composed of a representative from each department and the National Executive Committee, which includes the major national officers. Broad policy is established by the Convention and the Council, although the National Executive Committee has full power and authority to act for the association within the framework of organization mandates. Execution of the organization's policies falls in large measure to the professional staff housed in the ROA's national headquarters in Washington, D.C.[17] An executive director and directors of each of the three service sections guide the work of a staff numbering between twenty and twenty-five employees. Its current executive director is Colonel John T. Carlton, a man with military, newspaper, and Congressional staff experience.[18] Each of the three service directors had worked closely with reserve affairs as a career man in the armed forces before military retirement. As service directors in the ROA they continued to use this experience to help influence reserve forces policy. Although no salary is provided for the national president, about two-thirds of his time during his year in office is spent on organization affairs, including an extensive visitation program, the expenses for which he is reimbursed, and on liaison with the national staff.[19] In a practical way the necessity of personal resources limits the number of aspirants to the office to those who are able to sustain themselves financially while spending this time on the duties of the office.

Local chapters number almost 1,000 and are the closest association link with the individual reservists. Probably as much social as business activity is included in the chapter programs, and the intensity of activity varies greatly from one chapter to another. Occasionally chapters are based on reserve unit participation, in which case membership would be predominantly from one service. The ROA members overseas on active duty add to the geographical distribution of chapters. To finance both local and department activities, $2.75 out of the $8.00 annual dues is allocated to state and local units from the national headquarters, which retains the remaining $5.25 for its various operational expenses.[20]

At the state level periodic meetings of representatives from the chapters handle matters between annual department conventions.

At the national level the financial resources of the ROA are derived for the most part from that portion of annual dues allocated to the national headquarters.[21] According to the audit for the year ended March 31, 1964, over $270,000 of the $303,000 income was derived from dues. The remainder of the income was obtained from the sale of insignias and advertising in its magazine as well as from interest and dividends on relatively small investments. Expenses for the year were $308,000 with about two-thirds of the amount allocated to salaries and magazine publication. During that same year the land and building of its former office were sold for $100,000. Net worth of the organization was listed at slightly more than $400,000. The budget for the year ending March, 1965, was $481,000. Included in its assets were funds collected for its projected headquarters in the Capitol Hill area. In February, 1966, the new headquarters labeled the "Minuteman Memorial Building" moved a step nearer reality when a site at First Street and Constitution Avenue, across from the Senate Office Building, was purchased after hopes were abandoned for securing the necessary approvals for a building at the foot of Capitol Hill on Independence Avenue. About two-thirds of a $1.5 million building fund has been pledged and about half actually collected.

Membership figures for the ROA can be analyzed on several bases. By service, the Army still has the largest segment of the 57,553 total with 39,336. Other categories included: Air Force, 10,765; Navy, 6,088; Coast Guard, 1,131; Marine Corps, 203; and Public Health Service, 30.[22] In its life span the ROA has fluctuated greatly in total strength. At the end of its first year in 1923 the total was 3,830. A high of 140,000 was reached in 1947; and since the Berlin mobilization, total membership has remained under 60,000. Although these figures include officers in retired and extended active duty categories, the majority are in the Ready Reserve. About one-fifth of the ROA membership is on extended active duty on a career basis.

By state departments, California leads with 5,560 members, followed by New York with 4,405, while five of the least populated states have department memberships of less than 100. In October, 1963, a declining membership trend of several years' duration caused by the Berlin recall was reversed briefly. Since 1964 a slight net decrease in membership has occurred. Upon release from active duty, some officers drop out of reserve activity to avoid another recall. They usually drop their affiliation with the ROA at the same time if they have been members. The ROA feels that its membership potential is more than 700,000 in all services, of which 100,000 are in paid-drill units.

The ROA counts a significant number of congressmen among its members. Although it has claimed as many as 150 Congressional members in recent years, a check of the membership rolls in March, 1964, revealed sixty-five members from the Eighty-eighth Congress with current status in the ROA and forty-two with a recently expired membership. Forty-one of this combined total were in the Ready Reserve.[23] Since 1957 the ROA has had a Legislative Advisory Committee made up exclusively of congressmen who are also members of the ROA. This represented a decision to acknowledge openly the efforts of these Congressional members on behalf of the reserve components.[24] During the second session of the Eighty-eighth Congress, fourteen House and Senate members served with ROA's Legislative Advisory Committee under the chairmanship of Senator George Smathers, a Marine Corps Reserve colonel.[25] This group has been quite helpful to the ROA as an informal manager of bills relating to reserve interests.

In an organization structure oriented primarily to action at the national level, the professional staff and the National Executive Committee are intrusted with much of the responsibility for ROA activity. The Executive Committee meets at least quarterly to provide periodic guidance for the professional staff while the Association President is in more frequent contact with the Washington office. The tone of the organization is thus set largely by the national level. State departments and local chapters are less directly involved in the operation of the ROA. Resolutions from these levels eventually become the elements for broad guidance when they are approved by either the National Council or the Convention. Constituent units are especially urged and *do* convey to senators and representatives through personal contact the feelings of the Association on reserve policies. Dinner dances are frequently held by chapters, to which national, state, and local civilian and military officials are invited. In this way an attempt is made to cement rapport with political leaders as well as military commanders.

SETTING FOR ROA ACTIONS

Since World War II the ROA has been confronted by the growing assertion that American capability to meet its strategic commitments must be built on regular units backed up by an elite reserve force somewhat smaller than a large mobilization base of reservists. The ROA contended that the traditional dependence on a relativly small hard core of professional officers and a large civilian officer force was still valid. During the mid-1950's the strategy of a mobilization base was modified by a strategy of deterrence, which stressed readiness for almost immediate deployment. At the same time advances in weapons technology and force deployment methods required less personnel but demanded higher levels of training to develop proficiency. It became a question of whether reserve units could meet these requirements in any great numbers. There was the feeling that a reduction in numbers of reservists would permit the concentration of greater funds and time on those able to reach the levels of proficiency needed for a strategy of deterrence.

During this same postwar period the administration of the Department of Defense became increasingly centralized.[26] Beginning with the creation of a National Military Establishment in 1947, there has been a steady evolution toward centralization of control over defense activities. The Secretary of Defense has exercised direct control over major field commands of all services through the Joint Chiefs of Staff since 1958. Secretary of Defense McNamara has established central agencies to co-ordinate and, in fact, operate activities in logistics and intelligence that formerly had been left to the separate services.[27] As a consequence of these trends, the separate services have lost some of their independence in dealing with Congress and with interest groups. The ROA was still able to give counsel to the separate services, but it encountered reduced access at the Department of Defense level. With much of the initiative for military policy-making going to a growing Defense Department, Congress has still retained an important role in reserve affairs. The ROA assiduously cultivated a close working relationship with Congress in the committees dealing with reserve forces policy. Congressional committee chairmen who acquired expertise on military reserve affairs found themselves in great demand by military reserve associations throughout the postwar period.

An ever-present aspect of the environment in which ROA has operated has been the shadow cast by the National Guard Association. Under the fiery leadership of Major General Edward Walsh, the NGA made its aggressive presence felt after World War II. With the strong political base of state and local support, the NGA has been a most effective participant in the same legislative area with the ROA. The initial competition between the two organizations following World War II subsided, although it was never completely extinguished. More recently rivalry between the two groups has been aroused by the proposed merger of Army Reserve units into an expanded National Guard. The request for funds to handle the expansion of the Army National Guard at the expense of the Army Reserve will draw the ROA and the NGA into the same legislative ring as opponents.

The outlook of reserve officers has also conditioned the actions of the ROA. Two distinct outlooks about remaining in the reserve components beyond obligated time is encountered among officers. In one group were those who had been on active duty during World War II or the Korean conflict or both, and who, through personal commitment, desire for retirement benefits, or the interest in a military avocation, had become long-term, or hard-core, reservists hopeful of compiling twenty or more years of service. The other outlook is shared by many recent ROTC graduates who decide against a full-time military career and long-term reserve affiliation. They are desirous of severing relations with the armed forces as soon as their legal obligation is completed. Inextricably bound up in these outlooks is the conflict between the feeling of responsibility to prepare for service to country and the liberal spirit constantly wary of any tendencies toward extensive involvement in military activities.

Renewed emphasis on cost effectiveness and combat readiness in the Department of Defense has been a more recent feature of the military reserve setting. A complete review of all programs by Secretary McNamara has produced some proposals for change that have evoked some determined opposition.[28]

For example, the Secretary weighed the contribution of the reserve forces in terms of cost effectiveness and combat readiness and concluded that it was necessary to merge the two Army civilian components in order to reduce the overall, paid-drill strength.[29] Since the ROA interpretation of sufficient forces for adequate national defense was not the same as that found in the Secretary of Defense's proposals for a reduction in reserve forces, there has been continuous antagonism between the two.

MODE OF OPERATION

The strategy and tactics of the Reserve Officers Association have been based upon the strength of its resources and the setting in which it has operated. Its limited strength has caused a necessary concentration on items closest to reserve officers. The interpretation of its purpose to support a military policy that will provide adequate national security has been confined primarily to a concern for reserve personnel policy and to the maintenance of a large military reserve. Within this framework the ROA has sought to restrain administrative discretion in the enforcement of regulations by securing provisions in the reserve laws that give this protection.[30] In practice this has meant close ties with Congress and constant liaison with Pentagon offices.[31]

The ROA carefully watches all reserve legislation from its inception through final passage. More often than not it originates legislative proposals involving the reserve components in contrast to the procedure with respect to most military items that originate in the executive departments. Although the ROA is influential there is some evidence that more is claimed than should justly be credited to it. Close personal ties with Congressional leaders and the substantial segment of Congress associated with the reserve components have given the ROA opportunities to express its views and to secure approval for them. Testimony produced for reserve legislation occasionally sounds like the dialogue of a mutual admiration society. Besides testimony at hearings, participation by the ROA professional staff and elected officers in the "mark up" sessions, in which detailed changes are made in bills, has presented the ROA with the opportunity to translate organization proposals into specific legislative terms.[32] In a recent year the executive director and the service directors each spent almost one hundred days on the Hill at hearings and talking privately with over one hundred members of Congress.[33]

Publicizing recognition of Congressional efforts on behalf of ROA aims is accomplished through appointments and awards. Each year since 1958 the Legislative Advisory Committee has been composed of selected ROA members in Congress. In a sense they are managers of reserve legislation. A system of awards and citations, not necessarily limited to legislators, also focuses attention on the contributions of congressmen to the support of reserve forces.[34] Recipients over the last five years have included Senators Carl Hayden, Richard Russell, John Stennis, Margaret Chase Smith, and Dennis Chavez, and Representatives Carl Vinson, Mendel Rivers, Robert Sikes, and Edward Hébert.

The development of a close relationship between Congress and the ROA has led to charges of conflict of interest against congressmen who are either active reservists or members of the ROA. One consequence of these charges has been that congressmen in these categories have been afforded the unsolicited opportunity to proclaim their interest in national security and a willingness to share in the immediate task. Congressmen have defended their position by arguing that their intimate knowledge of reserve affairs through participation enables them to make better decisions on the issues related to reserve policies. The recent plan to remove congressmen from the Ready Reserve will undoubtedly affect their close working relationship with the ROA.[35]

The activities of ROA also involve liaison with various executive agencies before and after the introduction of legislative proposals on reserve forces policy. Some agreements between the military services and the ROA are worked out in advance as a means of satisfying a need without requesting a legislative proposal. A prior understanding between these groups also can prevent a public argument in front of a Congressional committee when a bill is being examined. The ROA staff directors for each service have close bonds with their respective services and these are carefully cultivated to achieve such agreements and understandings. In addition, regular officers are invited to participate in the ROA as associate members (without vote). This effort is aimed largely at major commanders to secure an official endorsement of reserve activities. The ROA also supports the requests for new equipment for regular forces with the hope that it will provide a "hardware fallout" for the reserve forces. The equipment replaced can then be given to reserve forces.

While the legislation is in process, frequent conferences between representatives of the ROA and the separate services are held. One of the services is usually designated as the agent to handle a legislative item for all three services. Since 1946 the antagonism between the regular and reserve elements has worn off, and when the regulars are unable to gain acceptance of a service recommendation at the Department of Defense level, they may try an "end run" through Congress with the help of members of the reserve components. Consequently, there seems to be mutual respect between the services and the ROA, but the Department of Defense has suspicions about the real interests of both groups, especially the latter. Access to service level offices for ROA is unrestricted, but the relationship of the ROA to the Department of Defense has changed considerably since 1946. The contrast is best illustrated when one considers that Secretary of Defense Louis Johnson made a personal appearance before the ROA National Convention in 1950, whereas at the most recent national convention, in 1964, the Secretary of Defense not only failed to send greetings but forwarded a filmed report about defense activities that made no mention of the reserve forces.[36]

After a reserve policy has been enacted into law, the difficult job remains of implementing the regulations for each of the services. The Reserve Officers Association has been active here by supporting the services when justified, by converting them to ROA interpretations when the occasion demands, or by objecting strenuously to any move that would prove detrimental. This is done in conference and personal discussion with officials directly involved in drawing up the regulations. If either a military department or other executive agency such as the Bureau of the Budget disagrees with the ROA on the manner of implementing a law, the ROA seeks additional support from Congress to secure the desired implementation.

Although most legislative situations can be handled satisfactorily by the ROA through the efforts of the national officers and staff, specific appeals to members for letters, telegrams, and telephone calls to congressmen have been successfully employed when the issue appeared in doubt. In commenting on the passage of the Reserve Officer Personnel Act by the House in 1953, the ROA magazine indicated:

> Departments, chapters and individual officers who responded to headquarters' "call to arms" deserve the highest praise. Members of the House were deluged with telegrams and phone calls urging support of ROPA. It was a perfect example of ROA at work on behalf of essential defense legislation.[37]

Attempts to build up broad public support by the ROA have had limited success. Sponsorship of National Defense Week to focus attention on the reserve components during the period between the birthdays of Lincoln and Washington was initiated to renew citizen interest in the National Defense Act of 1920. Testimonials by national leaders including the President could usually be expected. Another illustration is the manner in which the ROA was able to answer press criticism of the response of the Army's reserve components to the call to active duty during the Berlin crisis of 1961. To counter allegations of confusion and lack of readiness, the ROA gained rather wide attention with its "White Paper" answering the misconceptions, which it claimed constituted a national libel.[38]

Attempts to influence mass opinion have been very modest. The ROA national office does provide press releases on major reserve problems. The current merger proposal has stimulated a series of stories about the ROA. As a former newspaperman in Washington, the Executive Director has many friends among the press corps. In the past, John Ford, former Congressional Editor for the *Army Times*, and John G. Norris, Washington military analyst and columnist for the *Washington Post*, have made frequent contributions to the association magazine in addition to their writing for larger publics. State and local ROA units are encouraged to secure placement of stories in local papers about ROA activities including the presentation of awards to college ROTC units. Letters to the editor are another method that is used. But even when all of these activities are added together, the result is only a very slight impact on mass public opinion.

The ROA has worked mainly for legislation affecting the welfare of its own members. Being preoccupied with its own interests has not ruled out its co-operation with other groups. For example, it did work with the National Guard Association on reserve retirement legislation, but in 1952 some bitterness arose when the NGA withdrew its support for the Armed Forces Reserve Act. Both groups withstood the proposed reduction in paid-drill strength in 1958 and the years immediately following, but the proposal of Secretary of Defense McNamara on December 12, 1964, to merge Army Reserve and National Guard components under the National Guard has revived the rivalry between the two associations.

EFFECTIVENESS AND STATURE

Without implying that the ROA is solely responsible for whatever has been accomplished legislatively in the field of reserve forces policy, it is possible to point out certain broad goals of the ROA that also happen to have been incorporated into the national policy. Contingency plans evidently still allocate important missions to reserve forces since even the Department of Defense concedes the validity of the reserve concept, although in somewhat revised form. The authorized and programmed strengths of paid-drill units have remained quite stable in the face of a considerable number of threats. At the same time personnel policies essentially similar to ROA proposals have been enacted into law for drill pay, retirement benefits, promotion standards, categories of availability, and officer training. Numerous other measures for increased pay and special compensation have also been approved. A recent observer on the Washington scene attested to ROA effectiveness at least in part by stating that "citizen soldiers are so solidly entrenched politically that no one in Washington dares challenge them frontally."[39]

Despite the high esteem in which the ROA is held, it is still overshadowed by the National Guard Association. However, being second in a league that includes the NGA is not a small achievement. It may not be the sole spokesman for the Reserves, and it may have benefitted from NGA actions in the same area of legislation, but it is not a pale imitation of the NGA. Since 1946 the stature of the ROA has grown immensely.

THE ROA PATTERN AND INTEREST GROUP STUDY

What can be drawn from this analysis of the ROA pattern of activity that will add new dimensions to the conceptualization of interest groups in the American legislative process? Many of its characteristics and functions are found in other cases. It is not a large-scale group, but it is well organized. Its public is rather small in David Truman's sense and generally not easy to expand because the issues with which it deals are not of general interest.[40] Policy is directed by a relatively small group of leaders at the national level who are frequently defending the status of reserve forces.

Nor does the ROA's effective use of certain techniques significantly mark off the organization from other interest groups. Its ready access to influential legislators in its area of interest is acknowledged. Participation in informal negotiations by the ROA before the formal legislative process has begun has been a productive procedure.[41] Congressional sympathy for reserve forces has been carefully cultivated. ROA efforts in careful preparation of materials for internal consumption have the calculated effect of developing group cohesion.

The limitations of the ROA are those also found in other interest groups. It cannot hope to mobilize mass opinion on issues of such narrow scope as reserve affairs unless they are connected to principles involved in situations with more widespread appeal.[42] The resources of the ROA also limit the size of its demands. A major concern for personnel problems rather than weapons or strategy has confined its activity to work with only a few allied interest groups or segments of the American public. In competing with the Defense Department, the ROA also suffers from the handicap of not having all the information available to government agencies for policy recommendations.[43]

Perhaps the unique characteristic of the Reserve Officers Association is its hybrid nature of civilian and military in a society that ideally separates the two. Its membership cuts across social, economic, and political categories that would be distinguishing characteristics for other interest groups and in that sense is more pervasive. It is both civilian and military; it is partly private and partly public; and it is concerned with military affairs for all military services at the federal level. These factors give it a special status. This fusion of civilian and the military in the ROA makes it difficult to attack the organization. The possibility that the ROA can alter the traditional civil-military relationships in significant ways gives it an important place in the realm of interest group study.[44]

With this analysis of a prominent interest group in the field of reserve policy-making and the major cases that have occurred in the postwar era since 1946 completed, certain conclusions are now in order about the patterns of activity observed. These will be presented in the final chapter.

Footnotes

1. "Mac the Knife," *Newsweek*, December 21, 1964. When Secretary of Defense Robert McNamara proposed a merger of the two civilian components of the Army, it was indicated by this popular account that he took on two of the most powerful lobbies on Capitol Hill, the Reserve Officers Association and the National Guard Association. This gives some idea of the current stature of the ROA. Other

associations besides the National Guard Association have been involved in efforts to influence policy on reserve forces. These include the Air Force Association, the Fleet Reserve Association, the Retired Officers Association, the Naval Reserve Association, and the Marine Corps Reserve Officers Association.

2. Interviews with military personnel in charge of executive policy for the reserve forces were complimentary about the ROA. This conflicts in some degree with a general estimate by Jack Raymond in *Power at the Pentagon* (New York: Harper & Row, Publishers, 1964), p. 194, who stated: "Most of the Pentagon chiefs regard the Reserve organizations as more of a nuisance than an ally."

3. *Officer*, XXXIX (December, 1963), 26. President Truman's ties with ROA began in 1921 when he founded the local ROA chapter in Kansas City.

4. Reserve Officers Association of the United States, *ROA President's Manual*, n.d. (current), p. 3. Hereinafter cited as *ROA President's Manual*.

5. *Ibid.*, p. 4. General Reilly was a lecturer and writer who joined several friends in purchasing *Army, Navy Journal* and used it to aid the ROA's program.

6. *Reserve Officer*, IV (April, 1927), 7. The Thomason Act of 1935 provided training appointments for 1,000 officers, 50 of whom would get Regular Army commissions (49 *Stat.* 1028 [1935]).

7. *Ibid.*, XXVII (February, 1950), 13.

8. During the same period the Naval Reserve Officers Association, established in 1919, was active in gaining organized civilian support for a strong Naval Reserve. *Ibid.*

9. Norman Hapgood (ed.), *Professional Patriots* (New York: Albert & Charles Boni, 1927), pp. 11–12. Even its critics cited ROA as one of the active organizations fighting pacifiism.

10. Marcus Duffield, *King Legion* (New York: Jonathan Capi & Harrison Smith, 1931), p. 188. These two groups were successful in blocking public speeches by pacifists in many areas during the winter of 1926/27.

11. *Reserve Officer*, XVII (March, 1940), 7–8.

12. During World War II, while most of the members were on active duty, the Association was placed in the hands of a Board of Trustees, and all memberships (about 35,000 in 729 chapters) were frozen.

13. Separate service associations such as the Naval Reserve Association, the Air Force Association, and the Marine Corps Reserve Officers Association have continued to pursue highly specialized in-

terests with the separate services, but the ROA has worked with both single service problems as well as problems affecting all services.

14. 64 *Stat.* 312 (1950). An unsuccessful attempt to secure a national charter had been made in 1928. One of the benefits of such a charter aside from the status attached to it is that it obviates the need for each state department in the organization to secure a separate charter from the state in which it operates. Uniform auditing requirements for federally chartered corporations were established in 78 *Stat.* 635 (1964). This source also provides a list of the civic, patriotic, and philanthropic organizations chartered by Congress.

15. Each service section nominates a senior vice-president, a junior vice-president, and an executive committeeman who serves two years. Besides a president the Convention elects a judge advocate, three chaplains, a historian, a surgeon, and informal vice-presidents for the various theaters such as Europe, Asia, Antilles, and Central and South America.

16. *ROA President's Manual*, pp. 6–7. Informal regional caucuses at the National Convention tend to insure a broad geographical distribution of organization officers. In recent years Ready reservists have been assuming a more active role in association affairs. Retired and Standby reservists still have strong influence, however.

17. *Officer*, XL (December, 1964), 16–17. The present office facilities on Pennsylvania Avenue are regarded as temporary. In 1961 a memorial building drive was initiated under the direction of Lieutenant General Lewis B. Hershey, National Director of Selective Service. Construction of the Minuteman Memorial Building at Number one, Constitution Avenue, began in the fall of 1966.

18. Since World War II there have been three other executive directors: Brigadier General E. A. Evans, 1946–52; Colonel Charles M. Boyer, 1952–56; and Colonel Harold R. Duffie, 1956–57.

19. Major General James Frank, USAR, ROA National President for 1963–1964, interview on March 31, 1964. Expenses are handled by the ROA, but the National President frequently dips into his own pocket without expectation of reimbursement.

20. *ROA President's Manual*, p. 23.

21. *Officer*, XL (June, 1964), 28–29.

22. Selected membership figures for April, 1964, from a mimeographed distribution sheet at ROA national headquarters.

23. A recently announced plan of Secretary of Defense Robert McNamara to drop congressmen of the Ready Reserve from paid-drill status will also affect the number of congressmen in the ROA ("Drill Status Lost by Congressmen," *New York Times*, December 13, 1964, p. 84). Criticisms have been made from time to time of the alleged incompatibility of a congressman's holding a military commission.

One estimate indicated that 175 were in this category (John G. Norris, "Congress sans Reserve?", *Washington Post*, March 22, 1964, Section E, p. 3). One of the best known reserve units was Major General Barry Goldwater's 9999th Air Reserve Squadron. Another account claims that the wearing of the toga and the sword is plainly in violation of the Constitution and that new members of Congress were invited to join a reserve unit so that the services could gain easier access to them (Tristram Coffin, *The Passion of the Hawks* [New York: Macmillan Co., 1964], p. 186).

24. Jesse B. Stuart, "ROA Legislation as Seen from the Summit," *Officer*, XXXV (October, 1959), 8.

25. *Ibid.*, XXXIX (November, 1963), 11. Other members from the Senate with Reserve rank and component were: Colonel Ralph Yarborough, U.S. Army Reserve; Captain Hugh Scott, U.S. Naval Reserve; Colonel Gordon Allott, Air Force Reserve; Major General Barry Goldwater, AFRes; Major General Strom Thurmond, USAR; and Brigadier General Howard Cannon, AFRes. From the House were: Major General Robert Sikes, USAR; Colonel Stephen Derounian, USAR; Captain William S. Mailliard, USNR; Colonel Carl Albert, USAR; Captain Ray Roberts, USNR; Colonel Clement Zablocki, AFRes; and Commander Charles Chamberlain, U.S. Coast Guard Reserve. Senator Thurmond and Representative Sikes have been the most outspoken supporters of the ROA. Thurmond has a web of relationships with military and civilian personnel in government and private life who can be mobilized for support in times of stress for the Reserves. Sikes has key positions on the House Appropriations Subcommittees for Defense Activities and Military Construction.

26. John G. Norris, "Emergence of 'General Staff' Arouses Fear of Centralization at Pentagon," *Officer*, XXXVIII (October, 1962), 31; John Ford, "In 'Disneyland-East' Centralization Producing 'No Decision Trend' in Pentagon," *ibid.*, XXXIX (January, 1963), 24.

27. Hanson W. Baldwin, "Slow-down in the Pentagon," *Foreign Affairs*, XLIII (January, 1965), 262–64. See also John C. Ries, *The Management of Defense* (Baltimore: Johns Hopkins Press, 1964), p. 188.

28. Charles J. Hitch and Roland N. McKean, *Economics of Defense in the Nuclear Age* (Cambridge: Harvard University Press, 1960), pp. 315–20; William W. Kaufmann, *The McNamara Strategy* (New York: Harper & Row, 1964), pp. 173–83.

29. See note 1, *supra*.

30. J. M. Chambers, "You, ROA and Legislation," *Reserve Officer*, XXXII (May, 1956), 25.

31. Much of the material in this section is based on a group of interviews conducted, for the most part, during the winter and spring of 1964 only a few of which will be cited specifically. About thirty-five

people in all phases of legislative policy-making were interviewed. All are listed in the bibliography.

32. This procedure was carefully analyzed in Chapter IV dealing with the Reserve Officer Personnel Act.

33. John T. Carlton, "Across the Executive Desk," *Officer*, XXXIX (January, 1963), 10–11.

34. *ROA President's Manual*, pp. 30–31. The various categories include Minute Man of the Year, Minute Man Hall of Fame, Distinguished Service Citation, Outstanding Service Citation, and Award of Merit.

35. See note 23, *supra*.

36. This type of presentation left the clear impression that the effect was intended.

37. "ROA Washington Newsletter," *Reserve Officer*, XXIX (September, 1953), 1.

38. The report of General James Van Fleet acting as special consultant to President Kennedy backed up this position with laudatory comments on the reserve's performance during the Berlin buildup. A report of the House Armed Services Subcommittee investigating the recall placed the major share of blame on the faulty administration of the Army Reserve program. See *Officer*, XXXVIII (February, 1962), 8, 9, 27; and House Committee on Armed Services, *Report of Subcommittee No. 3 on Military Reserve Posture*, Committee Paper No. 70, 87th Cong., 2d sess., 1962, p. 6640. Another document making this point even more explicitly is a reoprt to the Congress by the Comptroller General of the United States entitled *Mismanagement and Ineffective Utilization of Ready Reserve Personnel in the XV Corps*, April 9, 1962 (B-148167). To the extent that reservists accepted and condoned these instances of poor management of the reserve program, they should share the responsibility for the readiness and performance standards uncovered by the Berlin recall. However, mismanagement of aspects of the reserve program would not seem to be a fair indictment of the value of the program or those in it. Regardless of the difficulties encountered during the recall period, the recall itself gave the Soviet Union a clear message of United States intent in Berlin.

39. Douglass Cater, *Power in Washington* (New York: Random House, 1964), p. 41.

40. David B. Truman, *The Governmental Process* (New York: Alfred A. Knopf, 1957), pp. 356–60.

41. This was pointed out at the state level by Gilbert Y. Steiner and Samuel K. Gove in *Legislative Politics in Illinois* (Urbana: University of Illinois Press, 1960), pp. 82–84.

42. A general formulation of the effect of the scope of conflict on the outcome may be found in E. E. Schattschneider, *The Semi-sovereign People* (New York: Holt, Rinehart & Winston, 1960), pp. 2–3.

43. This was not necessarily true of Army activities when Major General James E. Frank, USAR, was President of the ROA in 1963–64. As an Army reservist he was assigned as the Deputy to the Chief, Reserve Components, for his training. In such a position he became familiar with most of the plans for reserve forces.

44. A good, concise statement of the history of civil-military relationships in America can be found in Louis Morton's "Civilians and Soldiers: Civil-Military Relations in the United States," in William H. Nelson (ed.), *Theory and Practice in American Politics* (Chicago: University of Chicago Press for Rice University, 1964), pp. 123–37.

9

CONCLUSIONS
Legislative Imprint on Reserve Policy

9

CONCLUSIONS
Legislative Imprint on Reserve Policy

FROM THIS ANALYSIS of Congressional policy-making for the reserve forces for the period of the past twenty years, it is possible to draw some conclusions about developmental trends. In doing so, perhaps, the policy process of today can be clarified. Some short-range projections based on these conclusions will then be made. In short, I am hopeful of summarizing what the pattern of legislative policy-making for the reserve forces has been during the past two decades, what it is now, and what it will be in the near future. Then I want to compare briefly these conclusions with those reached in other studies.

DEVELOPMENTAL TRENDS

Throughout the past twenty years the federal reserve components have consistently received support from Congress, though that support may not always have been what the reserve components desired. In the key issues on which the maintenance of the reserve programs hinged, the national legislature made decisions that strengthened the programs. Near the end of the period under consideration a greater amount of strain existed in executive-legislative relations than in the beginning of the period. Congress encouraged interest group participation in this policy-making process as an alternate source of information. Issues within the reserve policy-making area were confined to narrow limits. In this respect the chairman of committees and subcommittees wielded a great deal of influence. The general public was not involved in reserve policy issues, and congressmen were less constrained in following their convictions or those of colleagues on the committees dealing with reserve problems. Partisan affiliation had little impact on decisions in the reserve area.

Executive department relations with Congress on reserve affairs has changed during the past two decades. The Chief Executive's attitude toward reserve affairs has been modified from one of close association and identification during Truman's time to initial enthusiasm and final frustration on the part of Eisenhower, to pressure for increased activity with fewer numbers under Kennedy, to, finally, a determined effort to curtail the role of reserve forces in national defense plans under Johnson. During this period relationships between the executive branch of government and Congress on reserve affairs has grown from one of almost full cooperation to that of sustained antagonism. Congress now faces a united effort from the Department of Defense in disagreements on reserve policy proposals. More frequently the matters under consideration dealt with civilian components of the Army rather than the other services because greater numbers of personnel, and hence more funds, were involved.

Congressional relationships with reserve interest groups changed very little during the past two decades. In the last three or four years, the National Guard Association has begun to work more closely with the Pentagon while still maintaining close ties with Congress. The Reserve Officers Association has grown in effectiveness during the same period. Although representatives of the ROA are no longer able to hammer out detailed legislative provisions in an executive session of a Congressional committee, the reputation and credibility of the organization is at an all-time high. From the standpoint of the ROA, the effort during the first decade of the twenty-year postwar period to secure legislative provisions for the reserve program placed it in an offensive role; the pressure was on the ROA to help produce laws. In the second decade the ROA was cast primarily in a defensive role attempting to protect the gains achieved for a viable reserve program. In the tactics of politics, playing the defensive role usually brings the advantage in legislative engagements, and the ROA is hopeful this will be the case in current controversies. The ideal held by reserve interest groups of getting program goals established in statute still prevails, and, to some degree, success in this area has removed some of the flexibility from the hands of military planners.[1]

During the postwar era greater awareness has developed among the general public for the role of citizen-soldier forces, but this has not been translated into any major clamor for action on various issues in reserve affairs. It is perhaps only a generalized feeling without being specifically related to the details of missions and capabilities. Publicity for reserve activities has not always been favorable, however. The reserve role in the Korean conflict was not questioned, but the complaints of some men called during the Berlin emergency in 1961 were hard to overcome with information on the effective response made by competent reservists. Since then a steady increase in the state of readiness has occurred to the point where some reserve units are approaching the status achieved by units of the regular forces.

During the past twenty years, elements in the civil-military relationship have also undergone some changes. It is now very difficult to secure the support of a senior professional military person for a reserve program that has not been approved by the civilian officials at the Department of Defense level. In the Truman administration, Congress and the reserve interest groups were able to count on direct support for reserve programs from professional military men regardless of Defense Department objectives and attitudes. With time has also come the general acceptance of the double standard for hard-core citizen-soldiers, which permits them to carry out official military duties and exercise full rights of political participation at the same time. In the past this has usually meant that the executive branch was unwilling to tackle any reduction or major reorganization of reserve forces for fear of political repercussions from the citizen-soldiers. Now the Department of Defense is willing to risk the trouble resulting from the introduction of various proposals to realign reserve forces with departmental goals. In twenty years we have moved from a situation in which the initiative for new policy came from the reserve elements, the professional military groups, or the Congress, to one in which the Department of Defense civilian leadership proposes changes for the reserve program, and Congress and reserve groups are pressed to disprove the merit of these proposals.

THE CONGRESSIONAL ROLE TODAY

In word and deed Congress retains today a primacy of interest in reserve affairs. Although Congress has insisted on exercising the final authority on reserve policy, it is now a somewhat more cautious protector of the reserve components. The National Guard and the exclusively federal reserve components are of equal concern to Congress, and this represents something of a gain for the position of the latter. As memories of World War II and the Korean conflict fade, those congressmen who were associated with these periods, either as servicemen or as lawmakers in the armed services area, become, perhaps, less susceptible to the appeal of reserve issues. Yet these issues represent an area in which the intention of Congress to regain some of the influence it has lost to executive ascendancy in national defense policy-making could be effected. Policy proposals in connection with reserve programs are given careful and detailed attention by Congress so that very specific guidance is provided to those who administer the statutes governing reserve activities.

Congressional relations with the executive branch involving reserve matters are now far from being cordial: they are, in fact, almost constantly antagonistic. The Department of Defense now assumes the offensive in initiating proposals for change in the reserve programs, frequently involving some reductions in personnel and expenditure. With a more centralized civilian direction emanating from the Pentagon, defense officials are more apt to challenge long-held notions about reserve components and traditional programs. Congressional reaction to this strong direction from the Department of Defense in executing as well as proposing legislation has been to complain that its intent in policy formulation is being violated.

The major reason for the growing gap between Congress and the Department of Defense on reserve policy is disagreement over the value of reserve forces in national defense plans. Since 1958 the Department of Defense has been trying to shift some of the resources from the reserve program to other defense programs. At the same time Congress has been blocking this proposed shift in resources. To support its position the Defense Department can muster data to show that the military requirements for a strategy of deterrence demand less investment in reservists on paid-drill status. For its judgment Congress can offer the evidence of previous emergencies in which a large number of reserve forces have been indispensable. Beyond these bases for judgments are other factors no doubt. The Department of Defense is concerned about the funding of reserve retirement pay as more and more reservists qualify through active reserve service, mainly through the paid-drill program. A stabilized paid-drill strength also permits the production and retention of reserve general officers who can exert an influence on reserve policy, in some instances in opposition to a Defense Department position. A steady base of numercial strength on which opposition can be built to decisions that might be unfavorable to reservists also reduces the flexibility that defense administrators might seek for their actions.

On the Congressional side another factor that might explain the differences of the Defense Department and Congress on reserve policy is the very real concern of congressmen to protect the economic interests of their constituents. Drill pay and other government expenditures required to support a reserve program add to the economic activity of an area, and its occupants are usually not happy to see curtailment of the reserve programs any more than they are to see the closing of defense installations.

Another reason for the current rise in executive-legislative tension in the reserve policy area is that the people holding key positions in each branch of government choose to interpret their roles in a very active sense—from the

President and the Secretary of Defense to the chairmen of Congressional committees dealing with defense affairs. In addition, little effort or intent to use tact is exhibited by either the Defense Department or Congress in approaching opposition when it develops on an issue. Consequently, each side presents about as uncompromising a position as is possible.

The questions in reserve policy are still relatively confined. The civil rights problem did enlarge the scope of the issue of the Junior ROTC program in high schools, and some hints were dropped that funds saved in the reserve area might be used in social welfare programs. For the most part, however, the reserve issues have remained within the domain of the armed services, which has given the Congressional chairmen in these areas an even greater amount of influence than is usual for them to have.

Having been nurtured by benevolent Congressional support, interest groups involved in reserve policy-making, such as the Reserve Officers Association, are now well stabilized in their operations and able to resist changes that are inimical to the personal welfare of their members. Yet congressmen are now beginning to show some reluctance to draw the bond of association as tight as it once was. However, Congress still seeks and finds information from the ROA that would otherwise not be uncovered. Thus, although Congress has created conditions that foster the development of articulate, organized interest groups which, in turn, reduce the flexibility in the administration of the reserve program, it has at the same time helped to preserve institutions that might otherwise be dismantled by the executive branch.

As much as Congress has exerted its efforts in the area of reserve policy-making, it still has not reached the stage where its function is primarily that of initiator. Its role is one of an emphatic monitor or reactor, since the first step is usually left to the executive side. Recently the proposals of the executive branch have provoked strong counterproposals from Congress, but unless the first move had come from the executive, the Congressional proposal probably would not have been forthcoming.

POLITICAL INFLUENCE OF CITIZEN-SOLDIERS

At the present time political activities of hard-core citizen-soldiers have assumed a defensive orientation. Although there is occasional criticism of reservists from the general public, proposals for change from the Department of Defense have been the dominant force in pushing reserve groups to a defensive stance. Usually the proposals call for a reduction in the number of personnel actively participating in the programs on a paid-drill status and the number of units assigned to the paid category. After years of sporadic criticism had been leveled at congressmen for continuing in an active reserve status while in office, they were finally removed from the Ready Reserve category in January, 1965, by a Department of Defense directive. The efforts to merge Army Reserve units into the National Guard involve reductions in the paid-drill strength. To combat these proposals for reductions in reserve programs reserve interest groups have been busy in a defensive role protecting the program wrought through legislative action in the first decade after World War II.

A summary of the key controversies in reserve affairs of the postwar period and the extent to which they were resolved in a manner favorable to the major groups of actors in the legislative arena is found in Table 2. The posi-

TABLE 2

ORGANIZATION POSITIONS ON RESERVE FORCES POLICY ISSUES, 1948–65*

POLICY ISSUE	MILITARY SERVICE(S)	DOD	ROA	NGA	CONGRESS
Reserve Retirement, 1948	O ➤ N	N	S	S	S
Armed Force Reserve Act of 1952	S	S	S	S ➤ N	S
Reserve Forces Act of 1955	S	S	S	O ➤ N	S
Reserve Officer Personnel Act of 1954–55	O ➤ S	O ➤ S	S	O ➤ S	S
Proposed Reduction in Paid-Drill Strength of Army Reserve Components, 1958–60	O	S	O	O	O
ROTC Vitalization Act of 1964	S	S	S	N	S
Proposal to Merge Army Reserve into Army National Guard	S	S	O	N ➤ S	O

*Key: S = Supported; O = Opposed; N = Took no position or neutral; ➤ = Change in Position; DOD = Department of Defense; ROA = Reserve Officers Association; and NGA = National Guard Association.

tion of the separate services was the official position of their departments, although reserve sections within each may have dissented privately or publicly. It might be argued that the National Guard Association was not as involved in matters that included all federal reserve components as it was in those dealing strictly with the Army or Air National Guard, such as items 5 and 7, and only in item 5 was its full political strength really committed. If not directly involved in most of the issues analyzed in this study, the National Guard still maintained a careful watch on them in the legislative process to see that its interests were not adversely affected. For the most part the type of policy issues chosen for careful analysis has been one in which those espousing reserve strength have tried to build and maintain both the total number of reservists and those in paid-drill status. The legislative acts selected from the first decade following World War II erected a statutory base on which reserve strength in the components of all services could be built. The second postwar decade saw a defensive action being staged largely by interest groups with the support of Congress to withstand attempts to reduce reserve strength.

Throughout the last two decades the political influence of the citizen-soldier has prevailed in the major policy issues selected for analysis. Whenever one of the two associations representing citizen-soldiers has differed with a Department of Defense proposal Congress has sustained association objections in considering that proposal for enactment. This pattern follows the contention of Charles Dale Story, at least in part. In referring to policy-making for the reserve components of only the Army in the first decade after World War II Story held that either the professional military group, the National Guard Association, or the Reserve Officers Association could exercise virtual veto authority if it opposed a policy proposal in the reserve forces area. In the last decade the veto condition has continued even when the Department of Defense and the National Guard Association have been in agreement on a policy proposal. However, Story's conclusion now applies only to the National Guard Association and the Reserve Officers Association. The third group, the professional military people, could probably have fitted into this concept until 1961. At that time the practice of career military personnel from the services going directly to Congress on reserve and other military matters to get help if the Department of Defense opposed their recommendations was curtailed.

With the exception of the merger proposal the ROA and the NGA have not actively pursued opposing positions. At the same time there has not been any close alliance promoting co-operative action on an issue on which both agree. The merger proposal has forced the two associations into opposing positions with the ROA fighting to save Army Reserve units. The chances of success for the merger proposal were improved with only one major association dissenting, but the plan still failed to gain the necessary Congressional support.

It is significant to point out that the position of the ROA was supported by Congress on each policy issue analyzed. Although the results cannot be explained completely by ROA influence, the pattern of success has been clear. From the ROA standpoint these were the most crucial issues for it in the postwar period, and its approach was one that attempted to force major reserve policy issues into the legislative arena where Congress could either erect a statuatory program favorable to ROA or else exert enough authority to block decisions that were regarded as unfavorable to the reserve programs.

The present reserve environment is a more difficult one for reserve interest groups to operate in, but they have adjusted quite well. Thinking primarily in terms of the Reserve Officers Association, the influence, accruing from its organizational resources and the past sympathetic concern of Congress, is being used very carefully. There is no big pressure action exerted on any reserve proposal but rather a quiet, thorough educational program to solicit Congressional support. Close relationships continue to be cultivated and maintained with the leaders of committees and subcommittees dealing with reserve affairs, but care is exercised to avoid antagonistic reactions from overselling or demanding exclusive endorsements. The sympathy of Congress for reserve interests is still easily aroused, but it must be supported with a well-documented case if the votes are to materialize in the showdown. Just as the military services have had to tool up to converse with systems analysts at the Department of Defense level, interest groups have had to research the replies to proposals for changes in reserve programs from the Defense Department in order to meet whatever challenge the proposals might offer to the current programs.

Perhaps if the new breed of aggressive analysts had not entered the Pentagon there would be some concern that domestic pressure from reserve interest groups would have their own way regardless of their effect on national defense strategies and cost. Today, however, the counterforce of the Pentagon has taken the initiative and put the reserve interest groups on the defensive, forcing them to justify all the programs receiving major outlays of funds. This leads to some conjecture about the future of reserve policy–making as far as legislative participation is concerned.

PROJECTIONS

Congressional activity in the reserve policy–making area will probably decline as the number of hard-core citizen-soldiers diminishes, largely through retirement. Within the next five years many of the reservists spawned by World War II and the Korean conflict will have left the reserve scene, but a wave of company grade officers will not have materialized as replacements for them. Active, organized interest groups will then come to focus more and more on the retirement policies of reservists by seeking to avoid any reduction in the programs now written into statute.

With some of the pressure to maintain active reserve forces removed, Congress will become more amenable to proposals for change from the Department of Defense. Matters of the reserve will tend to be considered more like those of the regular forces as far as Congress is concerned. If experience with limited wars continues as it has in the past, then less justification for maintaining a large reserve force will exist. It has taken a massive or a concentrated buildup of active duty forces to require the recall of reserve forces in the past generation. If the nation can continue to bar these two contingencies, then the move would be toward a much smaller reserve force. There are important values in the reserve force concept beyond its outright military capability that may cause some delay in its decline, but a more stabilized regular force complement of personnel with only a small active reserve force backup seems to be the direction of the future.

Just as the hard-core reservist is fading, so too are some of the Congressional stalwarts who built part of their careers in support of the reserve programs. The most prominent example would be that of Carl Vinson. The departure of others on the Senate side such as Leverett Saltonstall will also leave places not readily filled with the same degree of enthusiasm for the reserve program.

CORRELATION WITH OTHER STUDIES

When comparing this study with others completed on related aspects of Congressional activity, one can find points of both agreement and disagreement. Regarding the balance of power between Congress and the executive branch, the works of Raymond H. Dawson[2] and Joseph P. Harris[3] emphasize the methods used by Congress to curb executive action in national defense policy-making. Congressional action in the reserve affairs area tends to have the same restricting effect on the executive branch as Dawson shows in the case of authorization of appropriations for aircraft, missiles, and naval vessels and as Harris describes in the required approval of Congress for all military real estate transactions over the amount of $25,000.

From the standpoint of general public interest in national defense issues, this study could add reserve affairs to the list of such issues prepared by Lewis Dexter.[4] The contention of Dexter that there is very little public interest in most legislative policy decisions in the national defense area is confirmed in part by this study. On reserve affairs the legislator could feel that he had greater freedom to form conclusions and vote as "his own man" on reserve issues than on many others.

The influence of committee chairmen and committee decisions on the full House and Senate has been pervasive in the reserve force area. Professors E. E. Schattschneider[5] and Roland Young[6] both suggest that influence of chairmen and committees in issues of the reserve-force type is due in large measure to the restricted scope of those issues. The operation of this phenomenon is made more noticeable by the few exceptions. In the ROTC legislation of 1964, the subcommittee chairman lost his first bid to secure passage of the bill in the House because he could not overcome objections that the bill did not guarantee desegregated high school units in the junior division of the program. When the civil rights issue was handled by a separate act, the opposition to the ROTC bill wilted away.

The analyses of group influence in the legislative process have given rise to some differences over the reasons for its influence and the over-all impact on the democratic process. Martha Derthick's study of the National Guard Association tends to emphasize the favorable environment in which the Association was able to function as the major reason for its success in this field.[7] While the Reserve Officers Association operated in the same type of environment, the application of its own resources to the problems account for its success for the most part.

From the evidence of its operations and the nature of its impact on the legislative process, the ROA does not fit into the stereotyped model of the pressure group. That model portrays large and powerful organizations moving congressmen into line without regard for extensive documentation of their case. The early studies of Schattschneider[8] and E. Pendleton Herring[9] reflect a concern about the unequal power exhibited by pressure groups as compared with the general public and the possibilities for undermining the national interest. A more recent study by Charles Story on policy-making for the Army Reserve came to the somewhat similar conclusion that in national military policy the NGA, the ROA, and professional military groups might have too much influence on civilian leaders of the defense establishment and on the members of Congress.[10] This study saw no reason to be concerned about national interests being swept aside in order to provide benefits for a major interest group.

Instead, the findings of this research support the emphasis placed on the reciprocal nature of the relationship between interest groups and those they care to influence.[11] To conceptualize the influence process in this manner is to agree with the recent study by Bauer, Pool, and Dexter on foreign trade policy, which articulates the same theme with additional emphasis on the communication process.[12] In this sense the interest group becomes something of a service bureau for legislators by supplying carefully researched information helpful in solving problems in very specialized areas. Clapp confirms the desire of congressmen for straightforward talk from interest groups as the major reason for listening to them.[13] At the state level Wahlke and his associates discovered the same value of the information function of interest groups.[14] In this sense the Reserve Officers Association has served as a reservoir of data backed up by experience and as a source of specific recommendations in reserve legislation. Its members serve on active duty and observe the military situation at close hand while its permanent staff in Washington follows governmental developments at the top. At the same time the ROA has found its goals modified by friendly congressmen and some of its efforts used to assist them in the development of a national reputation.

CLOSING

Issues in reserve affairs have persistently claimed the attention of Congress as it has been involved in national defense policy-making. For its part Congress has shown a primacy of interest in the reserve program and has exerted exceptional efforts to impress the executive branch of government with Congressional authority in this field. These efforts by Congress have been encouraged by citizen-soldiers acting individually and through effective political interest groups. Although the reserve concept has survived as an element of national security, its character has changed in the direction of greater readiness of deployment. Congress and the citizen-soldier have developed a successful alliance in reserve affairs that has added to the prestige and influence of both.

Footnotes

1. The decision by President Johnson in July, 1965, to increase the draft quotas rather than call up the reserves to provide additional forces for Vietnam may have been influenced to some degree by the greater flexibility offered by the former in adjusting United States

military strength to the level required for a limited conflict. The reasoning behind this is that activation of procedures for recall established by statute tend to be construed as a mobilization, a hardened escalation, which would reduce the credibility of the United States goal of limited aims in Vietnam.

2. Raymond H. Dawson, "Innovation and Intervention in Defense Policy," in Robert L. Peabody and Nelson W. Polsby (eds.), *New Perspectives on the House of Representatives* (Chicago: Rand McNally & Co., 1963), p. 302.

3. Joseph P. Harris, *Congressional Control of Administration* (Washington, D.C.: Brookings Institution, 1964), pp. 219–25.

4. Lewis Anthony Dexter, "Congress and the Making of Military Policy," in Peabody and Polsby, *op. cit.*, pp. 307–8.

5. E. E. Schattschneider, *The Semisovereign People* (New York: Holt, Rinehart & Winston, 1960), pp. 3–5.

6. Roland Young, *The American Congress* (New York: Harper & Bros., 1958), p. 159.

7. Martha Derthick, *The National Guard in Politics* (Cambridge, Mass.: Harvard University Press, 1965), pp. 164–65.

8. E. E. Schattschneider, *Politics, Pressures and the Tariff* (New York: Prentice-Hall, 1935), p. 288.

9. E. Pendleton Herring, *Group Representation Before Congress* (Baltimore: Johns Hopkins Press, 1929), pp. 241–42.

10. Charles Dale Story, "The Formulation of Army Reserve Forces Policy: Its Setting amidst Pressure Group Activity" (unpublished Ph.D. dissertation, University of Oklahoma, 1958), p. 275.

11. Harmon Zeigler, *Interest Groups in American Society* (Englewood Cliffs, N.J.: Prentice-Hall, 1964), p. 270.

12. Raymond A. Bauer, Ithiel de Sola Pool, and Lewis Anthony Dexter, *American Business and Public Policy* (New York: Atherton Press, 1963), p. 353.

13. Charles L. Clapp, *The Congressman: His Work as He Sees It* (Washington, D.C.: Brookings Institution, 1963), p. 162.

14. John C. Wahlke and others, *The Legislative System* (New York: John Wiley & Sons, 1962), pp. 338–39.

BIBLIOGRAPHY

BIBLIOGRAPHY

BOOKS

Army Almanac, The. Harrisburg, Pa.: Stackpole Co., 1959.

BAILEY, STEPHEN KEMP. *Congress Makes a Law.* New York: Columbia University Press, 1950.

BAUER, RAYMOND A.; POOL, ITHIEL DE SOLA; and DEXTER, LEWIS ANTHONY. *American Business and Public Policy.* New York: Atherton Press, 1963.

BERMAN, DANIEL M. *In Congress Assembled.* New York: Macmillan Co., 1964.

BERNARDO, C. JOSEPH, and BACON, EUGENE H. *American Military Policy: Its Development since 1775.* Harrisburg, Pa.: Stackpole Co., 1961.

BLAISDELL, DONALD C. *American Democracy under Pressure.* New York: Ronald Press Co., 1957.

BROWNLEE, JAMES F. *The Defense We Can Afford.* New York: Committee on Economic Development, 1958.

BURNS, JAMES MACGREGOR. *Congress on Trial.* New York: Harper & Row, 1949.

CATER, DOUGLAS. *Power in Washington.* New York: Random House, 1964.

CHAMBERLAIN, LAWRENCE H. *The President, Congress, and Legislation.* New York: Columbia University Press, 1946.

CLAPP, CHARLES L. *The Congressman: His Work as He Sees It.* Washington, D.C.: Brookings Institution, 1963.

COFFIN, TRISTRAM. *The Passion of the Hawks.* New York: Macmillan Co., 1964.

COLES, HARRY L. (ed.). *Total War and Cold War: Problems in Civilian Control of the Military.* Columbus: Ohio State University Press, 1962.

COOK, FRED J. *The Warfare State.* New York: Macmillan Co., 1962.

DERTHICK, MARTHA. *The National Guard in Politics.* Cambridge, Mass.: Harvard University Press, 1965.

DUFFIELD, MARCUS. *King Legion.* New York: Jonathan Capi and Harrison Smith, 1931.

ECCLES, HENRY E. *Military Concepts and Philosophy.* New Brunswick, N. J.: Rutgers University Press, 1965.

EKIRCH, ARTHUR A., JR. *The Civilian and the Military.* New York: Oxford University Press, 1956.

ELIOT, GEORGE FIELDING. *Reserve Forces and the Kennedy Strategy.* Harrisburg, Pa.: Stackpole Co., 1962.

FINER, S. E. *The Man on Horseback.* New York: Frederick A. Praeger, 1962.

FOOT, M. R. D. *Men in Uniform.* New York: Frederick A. Praeger, 1961.

FROMAN, LEWIS A., JR. *Congressmen and Their Constituencies.* Chicago: Rand McNally & Co., 1963.

FRYE, WILLIAM. *Marshall: Citizen Soldier.* New York: Bobbs-Merrill Co., 1947.

GALLOWAY, GEORGE B. *The Legislative Process in Congress.* New York: Thomas Y. Crowell Co., 1953.

GANOE, WILLIAM ADDLEMAN. *The History of the United States Army.* New York: D. Appleton-Century, 1924.

GELLERMAN, WILLIAM. *The American Legion as Educator.* New York: Teachers College, Columbia University, 1938.

GRAY, JUSTIN. *The Inside Story of the Legion.* New York: Boni & Gaer, 1948.

GRIFFITH, ERNEST S. *Congress, Its Contemporary Role.* 3d ed. New York: New York University Press, 1961.

GROSS, BERTRAM M. *The Legislative Struggle.* New York: McGraw-Hill Book Co., 1953.

HAMMOND, PAUL Y. *Organizing for Defense.* Princeton: Princeton University Press, 1961.

HAPGOOD, NORMAN (ed.). *Professional Patriots.* New York: Albert & Charles Boni, 1927.

HARRIS, JOSEPH P. *Congressional Control of Administration.* Washington, D.C.: Brookings Institution, 1964.

HERRING, E. PENDLETON. *Group Representation before Congress.* Baltimore: Johns Hopkins Press, 1929.

———. *The Impact of War.* New York: Farrar & Rinehart, 1941.

———. *Public Administration and the Public Interest.* New York: McGraw-Hill Book Co., 1936.

HILL, JIM DAN. *The Minute Man in Peace and War.* Harrisburg, Pa.: Stackpole Co., 1964.

HITCH, CHARLES J. *Decision-Making for Defense.* Berkeley and Los Angeles: University of California Press, 1965.

HITCH, CHARLES J., and MCKEAN, ROLAND N. *Economics of Defense in the Nuclear Age.* Cambridge: Harvard University Press, 1960.

HOWARD, MICHAEL (ed.). *Soldiers and Governments.* Bloomington: Indiana University Press, 1959.

HUNTINGTON, SAMUEL P. *The Common Defense.* New York: Columbia University Press, 1961.

———. *The Soldier and the State.* Cambridge: Belknap Press of Harvard University Press, 1959.

HUZAR, ELIAS. *The Purse and the Sword.* Ithaca, N.Y.: Cornell University Press, 1950.

JANOWITZ, MORRIS. *The Professional Soldier.* Glencoe, Ill.: Free Press of Glencoe, 1960.

———. *Sociology and the Military Establishment.* New York: Russell Sage Foundation, 1959.

KAUFMANN, WILLIAM W. *The McNamara Strategy.* New York: Harper & Row, 1964.

KEEFE, WILLIAM J. and OGUL, MORRIS S. *The American Legislative Process.* Englewood Cliffs, N.J.: Prentice-Hall, 1964.

KERWIN, JEROME (ed.). *Civil-Military Relationships in American Life.* Chicago: University of Chicago Press, 1948.

KINTNER, WILLIAM R. *Forging a New Sword.* New York: Harper & Bros., 1958.

KOFMEHL, KENNETH. *Professional Staffs of Congress.* West Lafayette, Ind.: Purdue Research Foundation, 1962.

LATHAM, EARL. *The Group Basis of Politics.* Ithaca, N.Y.: Cornell University Press, 1952.

LODGE, HENRY CABOT (ed.). *The Federalist.* New York: G. P. Putnam's Sons, 1888.

LYONS, GENE M., and MASLAND, JOHN W. *Education and Military Leadership.* Princeton: University Press, 1959.

MCBRIDE, JAMES H., and EALES, JOHN I. H. (eds.). *Military Posture: Fourteen Strategic Issues before Congress 1964.* New York: Praeger, 1965.

MACNEIL, NEIL. *Forge of Democracy.* New York: David McKay Co., 1963.

MAHON, JOHN K. *The American Militia: Decade of Decision, 1789–1800.* Gainesville: University of Florida Press, 1960.

MASLAND, JOHN W., and RADWAY, LAWRENCE I. *Soldiers and Scholars.* Princeton: Princeton University Press, 1957.

MILBRATH, LESTER W. *The Washington Lobbyists.* Chicago: Rand McNally & Co., 1963.

MILLIS, WALTER. *Arms and Men.* New York: G. P. Putnam's Sons, 1956.

MILLIS, WALTER (ed.). *The Forrestal Diaries.* New York: Viking Press, 1951.

MILLIS, WALTER, with MANSFIELD, HARVEY C., and STEIN, HAROLD. *Arms and the State: Civil-Military Elements in National Policy.* New York: Twentieth Century Fund, 1958.

MILLS, C. WRIGHT. *The Causes of World War III.* New York: Simon & Schuster, 1958.

———. *The Power Elite.* New York: Oxford University Press, 1956.

National Guard Association. *Our Nation's National Guard.* Washington, D.C. National Guard Association, 1954.

NEBLETT, WILLIAM H. *No Peace with the Regulars.* New York: Pageant Press, 1957

———. *Pentagon Politics.* New York: Pageant Press, 1953.

ODEGARD, PETER H. *Pressure Politics.* New York: Columbia University Press, 1928.

OSTHEIMER, RICHARD H. *Student Charges and Financing Higher Education.* New York: Columbia University Press, 1953.

PALMER, JOHN MCAULEY. *America in Arms.* New Haven: Yale University Press, 1941.

RAYMOND, JACK. *Power at the Pentagon.* New York: Harper & Row, 1964.

RIES, JOHN C. *The Management of Defense.* Baltimore: Johns Hopkins Press, 1964.

RIKER, WILLIAM H. *Soldiers of the States.* Washington, D.C.: Public Affairs Press, 1957.

SALOMA, JOHN S., III. *The Responsible Use of Power.* Washington, D.C.: American Enterprise Institute, 1964.

SCHATTSCHNEIDER, E. E. *Politics, Pressures and the Tariff.* New York: Prentice-Hall, 1935.

———. *The Semisovereign People.* New York: Holt, Rinehart & Winston, 1960.

SCHILLING, WARNER R.; HAMMOND, PAUL Y.; and SNYDER, GLENN H. *Strategy, Politics, and Defense Budgets.* New York: Columbia University Press, 1962.

SHARFF, LEE F. (ed.). *Uniformed Services Almanac, 1964.* Washington, D.C.: Federal Employees' News Digest, 1964.

SMITH, DALE O. *U.S. Military Doctrine.* New York: Duell, Sloan & Pierce, 1955.

SMITH, LOUIS. *American Democracy and Military Power.* Chicago: University of Chicago Press, 1951.

Social Science Research Council, Committee on Civil-Military Relations Research. *Civil-Military Relations (An Annotated Bibliography, 1940–1952).* New York: Columbia University Press, 1954.

STANLEY, TIMOTHY N. *American Defense and National Security.* Washington, D.C.: Public Affairs Press, 1956.

STEINER, GILBERT Y., and GOVE, SAMUEL K. *Legislative Politics in Illinois.* Urbana: University of Illinois Press, 1960.

STERN, FREDERICK MARTIN. *The Citizen Army.* New York: St. Martin's Press, 1957.

STIMSON, HENRY L., and BUNDY, MCGEORGE. *On Active Service in Peace and War.* New York: Harper & Bros., 1948.

SWOMLEY, JOHN M., JR. *The Military Establishment.* Boston: Beacon Press, 1964.

TAYLOR, MAXWELL D. *The Uncertain Trumpet.* New York: Harper & Bros., 1959.

THOMAS, NORMAN C., and LAMB, KARL A. *Congress, Politics and Practice.* New York: Random House, 1964.

TRUMAN, DAVID B. *The Governmental Process.* New York: Alfred A. Knopf, 1957.

TRUMAN, HARRY S. *Memoirs, I, Year of Decisions.* Garden City, N.Y.: Doubleday & Co., 1955.

————. *Memoirs, II, Years of Trial and Hope.* New York: Doubleday & Co., 1956.

WAHLKE, JOHN C.; EULAU, HEINZ; BUCHANAN, WILLIAM; and FERGUSON, LEROY. *The Legislative Process.* New York: John Wiley & Sons, 1962.

WALLACE, ROBERT ASH. *Congressional Control of Federal Spending.* Detroit: Wayne State University Press, 1960.

War Reports of General of the Army George C. Marshall, General of the Army H. H. Arnold, and Fleet Admiral Ernest King, The. New York: J. B. Lippincott Co., 1947.

WEIGLEY, RUSSELL F. *Towards An American Army.* New York: Columbia University Press, 1962.

WILDAVSKY, AARON. *The Politics of the Budgetary Policy.* Boston: Little, Brown & Co., 1964.

YOUNG, ROLAND. *The American Congress.* New York: Harper & Bros., 1958.

ZEIGLER, HARMON. *Interest Groups in American Society.* Englewood Cliffs, N.J.: Prentice-Hall, 1964.

ARTICLES AND PERIODICALS

ALMOND, GABRIEL A. "A Comparative Study of Interest Groups and the Political Process," *American Political Science Review,* LII (March, 1958), 270–82.

ALSOP, STEWART. "Our New Strategy: The Alternatives to Total War," *Saturday Evening Post,* CCXXXVI (December 1, 1962), 13–18.

BALDWIN, HANSON W. "Slow-Down in the Pentagon," *Foreign Affairs,* XLIII (January, 1965), 262–80.

BECTON, JULIAN. "The Naval Reserve Today," *Naval Review, 1964.* Annapolis, Md.: U.S. Naval Institute, pp. 242–65.

BURDETTE, FRANKLIN. "Congress, the People, and Administration," *Public Administration Review,* XXIV (December, 1965), 259–65.

COCHRANE, JAMES D. "Partisan Aspects of Congressional Committee Staffing," *Western Political Quarterly,* XVI (June, 1964), 338–48.

COLLINS, FREDERICK W. "Military Indoctrination of Civilians," *New Republic,* CXLIV (June 26, 1961), 13–14.

Congressional Quarterly Almanac. 1947–62.

CONN, STETSON. "Changing Concepts of National Defense in the United States, 1937–47," *Military Affairs,* XXVIII (Spring, 1964), 1–7.

DAWSON, RAYMOND H. "Innovation and Intervention in Defense Policy," in ROBERT L. PEABODY and NELSON W. POLSBY (eds.), *New Perspectives on the House of Representatives.* Chicago: Rand McNally & Co., 1963, pp. 273–303.

DERTHICK, MARTHA ANN. "Militia Lobby in the Missile Age—The Politics of the National Guard," in SAMUEL P. HUNTINGTON (ed.), *Changing Patterns of Military Politics.* New York: Free Press of Glencoe, 1962, pp. 190–232.

DEXTER, LEWIS ANTHONY. "Congressmen and the Making of Military Policy," in ROBERT L. PEABODY and NELSON W. POLSBY (eds.), *New Perspectives on the House of Representatives.* Chicago: Rand McNally & Co., 1963, pp. 305–24.

DODDS, HAROLD W. "Your Boy and the ROTC," *Atlantic Monthly,* CXCI (March, 1953), 25–29.

ELDERSVELD, SAMUEL J. "American Interest Groups: A Survey of Research and Some Implications for Theory and Method," in HENRY W. EHRMANN (ed.), *Interest Groups on Four Continents.* Pittsburgh: University of Pittsburgh Press, 1958, pp. 173–96.

ELIOT, GEORGE FIELDING. "The Conflict in the Pentagon," *American Legion,* LXXV (November, 1963), 8–9, 41.

ENTHOVEN, ALAIN C. "Choosing Strategies and Selecting Weapons," *U.S. Naval Institute Proceedings,* XC (January, 1964), 150–58.

FENNO, RICHARD F., JR. "The House Appropriations Committee as a Political System: The Problem of Integration," *American Political Science Review,* LVI (June, 1962), 310–24.

FITZPATRICK, EDWARD A. "The Volunteer and the Conscript in American Military History," *Current History*, XXXVIII (April, 1960), 205–13.

FOX, WILLIAM T. R. "Civilians, Soldiers, and American Policy," *World Politics*, VII (April, 1965), 402–18.

————. "Civil-Military Relations Research," *World Politics*, VI (January, 1954), 278–88.

FRIEDMAN, SAUL. "The Rand Corporation and Our Policy Makers," *Atlantic Monthly*, CCXII (September, 1963), 61–68.

GABLE, RICHARD W. "Interest Groups as Policy Shapers," *Annals*, CCCXIX (September, 1958), 84–93.

GARCEAU, OLIVER. "Interest Group Theory in Political Research," *Annals*, CCCXIX (September, 1958), 104–12.

GILPATRICK, ROSWELL L. "Our Defense Needs: The Long View," *Foreign Affairs*, XLII (April, 1964), 366–78.

GINSBURGH, ROBERT N. "The Challenge to Military Professionalism," *Foreign Affairs*, XLII (January, 1964), 255–68.

HANNAH, JOHN A. "Manpower for Defense," *State Government*, XXVII (January, 1954), 6–10.

HOLLAND, CECIL. "Call-up of Army Reserve Studied to Meet Shortages," *Washington Star*, April 28, 1966, p. 1.

HOOPES, TOWNSEND. "Civilian-Military Ballance," *Yale Review*, XLIII (December, 1953), 218–34.

HOWARD, MICHAEL. "Civil-Military Relations in Britain and the U.S., 1945–1958," *Political Science Quarterly*, LXXV (March, 1960), 35–46.

HUNTER, ROBERT E. "The Politics of U.S. Defense, 1963," *World Today*, XIX (April, 1963), 155–66.

HUNTINGTON, SAMUEL P. "Civilian Control and the Constitution," *American Political Science Review*, L (September, 1956), 676–99.

————. "Civilian Control of the Military: A Theoretical Statement," in HEINZ EULAU, SAMUEL J. ELDERSVELD, and MORRIS JANOWITZ (eds.), *Political Behavior: A Reader in Theory and Method.* Glencoe, Ill.: Free Press of Glencoe, 1956, pp. 380–85.

————. "Congressional Response to the Twentieth Century," in *Congress and America's Future.* Englewood Cliffs, N.J.: Prentice-Hall, 1965.

————. "Equilibrium and Disequilibrium in American Military Policy," *Political Science Quarterly*, LXXVI (December, 1961), 481–502.

————. "Interservice Competition and the Political Roles of the Armed Services," *American Political Science Review*, LV (March, 1961), 40–52.

————. "Men at Arms?", *Columbia University Forum*, II (Spring, 1959), 42–47.

————. "Power, Expertise, and the Military Profession," *Daedalus* LCII (Fall, 1964), 785–807.

JOHNSON, MAX S. "McNamara: The Real Story: A Military Expert's Appraisal of Revolution in the Pentagon and the Role of Defense Secretary Robert S. McNamara," *U.S. News and World Report*, LV (July 22, 1963), 56–59.

Journal of the Armed Forces. (Replaced the *Army, Navy, Air Force Journal & Register* in June, 1964.), 1964.

KELLY, GEORGE A. "Officers, Politics, Ideology," *Army*, XII (January, 1962), 30–33.

KNEBEL, FLETCHER, and BAILEY, CHARLES W. "Military Control: Can It Happen Here?", *Look* XXVI (September 11, 1962), 17–22.

KOLODZIEJ, E. A. "Congressional Responsibility for the Common Defense: The Money Problem," *Western Political Quarterly*, XVI (March, 1963), 149–60.

LOWE, GEORGE E. "The Specter of a 'Man on Horseback'," *U.S. Naval Institute Proceedings*, XC (January, 1964), 26–35.

LOWI, THEODORE. "American Business Public Policy, Case Studies, and Political Theory," *World Politics* XVI (July, 1964), 677–715.

LYONS, GENE M. "The Growth of National Security Research," *Journal of Politics*, XXV (August, 1963), 489–508.

————. "The Military Mind," *Bulletin of the Atomic Scientists*, XIX (November, 1963), 19–22.

————. "The New Civil-Military Relations," *American Political Science Review*, LV (March, 1961), 53–63.

MANSFIELD, HARVEY C. "Civil-Military Relations in the U.S.," *Current History*, XXXVIII (April, 1960), 228–33.

MARSHALL, S. L. A. "McNamara's Latest Reform, Why His National Guard Scheme Won't Work," *New Republic*, CLII (January 23, 1965), 13–15.

MASSEY, ROBERT J. "Program Packages and the Program Budget in the Department of Defense," *Public Administration Review*, XXIII (March, 1963), 30–34.

McCONAUGHY, JAMES L., JR. "Effectiveness of Congress in Military Affairs: How Good Is the Record?", *Fortune*, LVII (April, 1958), 160.

McNAMARA, ROBERT S. "Managing the Department of Defense," *Civil Service Journal*, IV (April-June, 1964), 1–5.

MORTON, LOUIS. "Civilians and Soldiers: Civil-Military Relations in the United States," in WILLIAM H. NELSON (ed.), *Theory and Practice in American Politics*. Chicago: University of Chicago Press for Rice University, 1964, pp. 123–37.

MURPHY, CHARLES J. V. "The Embattled Mr. McElroy," *Fortune*, LIX (April, 1959), 147–50.

NIELSON, WALDMAR A. HUGH. "Hidden Impact of the Pentagon," *New York Times Magazine*, June 25, 1961, pp. 9, 31–36.

NORRIS, JOHN G. "Congress Sans Reserve?", *Washington Post*, March 22, 1964, Section E, p. 3.

OBERDORFER, DON. "Rivers Delivers," *New York Times Magazine*, August 29, 1965, p. 31.

PACKMAN, MARTIN. "Military Manpower," *Editorial Research Reports*, June 3, 1954, pp. 399–418.

POSVAR, WESLEY W. "National Security Policy: The Realm of Obscurity," *Orbis*, IX (Fall, 1965), 694–713.

PYE, LUCIAN W. "Effects of Legislative and Administrative Accessibility on Interest Group Politics," *PROD*, I (January, 1958), 11–14.

RAPAPORT, DAVID C. "A Comparative Theory of Military and Political Types," in SAMUEL P. HUNTINGTON (ed.), *Changing Patterns of Military Politics*. New York: Free Press of Glencoe, 1962, pp. 77–96.

RAYMOND, JACK. "The Draft Is Unfair," *New York Times Magazine*, January 2, 1966, pp. 5 ff.

ROBINSON, DONALD. "Does the Army Want the Reserves?," *Colliers*, CXXI (April 10, 1948), 24–25, 68.

St. Louis Post Dispatch, October 24, 1965.

SCHER, SEYMOUR. "Conditions for Legislative Control," *Journal of Politics*, XXV (August, 1963), 526–51.

SENTER, RAYMOND D. "The Dilemma of the Military," *Bulletin of the Atomic Scientists*, XIX (December, 1963), 24–27.

SOUERS, SIDNEY W. "Policy Formulation for National Security," *American Political Science Review*, XLIII (June, 1949), 534–43.

STEEL, RONALD. "Is Congress Obsolete?", *Commentary*, XXXVIII (September, 1964), 59–64.

STEMPEL, JOHN D. "The Selected Reserve—Problems in Readiness," *U.S. Naval Institute Proceedings*, LXXXIX (August, 1963), 100–102.

TARR, DAVID W. "The American Military Presence Abroad," *Orbis*, IX (Fall, 1965), 630–54.

TRUMAN, HARRY S. "Our Armed Forces Must Be Unified," *Colliers*, CXVII (August 26, 1944), 16, 63–64.

U.S. Code Congressional and Administrative News.

VAN RIPER, PAUL P. "A Survey of Materials for the Study of Military Management," *American Political Science Review*, IL (September, 1955), 828–50.

WILHELM, ROSS. "How to End the Draft," *Nation*, CCI (November 15, 1965), 350–52.

WITMER, T. RICHARD. "The Aging of the House," *Political Science Quarterly*, LXXIX (December, 1964), 527–37.

WORSNOP, RICHARD L. "Reserve Forces and the Draft," *Editorial Research Reports*, January 20, 1965, pp. 43–60.

PUBLIC DOCUMENTS

Budget of the United States Government for the Fiscal Year Ending June 30, 1950. Washington, D.C.: Government Printing Office, 1949.

Budget of the United States Government for the Fiscal Year Ending June 30, 1959. Washington, D.C.: Government Printing Office, 1958.

Budget of the United States Government for the Fiscal Year Ending June 30, 1960. Washington, D.C.: Government Printing Office, 1959.

Budget of the United States Government for the Fiscal Year Ending June 30, 1961. Washington, D.C.: Government Printing Office, 1960.

Budget of the United States Government for the Fiscal Year Ending June 30, 1964. Washington, D.C.: Government Printing Office, 1963.

Comptroller-General of the United States. *Annual Report, 1962.* Washington, D.C.: Government Printing Office, 1962.

Comptroller-General of the United States. *Mismanagement and Ineffective Utilization of Ready Reserve Personnel in the XV Corps.* Report to the Congress, April 9, 1962 (B-148167).

DONNELLY, CHARLES H. *United States Defense Policies since World War II.* H. Doc. No. 100, 85th Cong., 1st sess., 1957.

————. *United States Defense Policies in 1957.* H. Doc. No. 436, 85th Cong. 2d sess., 1958.

————. *United States Defense Policies in 1958.* H. Doc. No. 227, 86th Cong., 1st sess., 1959.

————. *United States Defense Policies in 1959.* H. Doc. No. 432, 86th Cong., 2d sess., 1960.

National Guard Bureau. Office of Public Affairs. *Retirement Policy for Guardsmen.* Washington, D.C.: Government Printing Office, 1959.

National Security Training Commission. *20th Century Minutemen.* A Report to the President. Washington, D.C.: Government Printing Office, December 1, 1953.

Office of Defense Mobilization. *Manpower Resources for National Security.* A Report to the President by the Director. Washington, D.C.: Government Printing Office, January 6, 1954.

TANSILL, WILLIAM R. *The Concept of Civil Supremacy over the Military in the United States.* Washington, D.C.: Legislative Reference Service, Library of Congress, February, 1951.

U.S. Department of Defense (National Military Establishment). *First Report of the Secretary of Defense.* Washington, D.C.: Government Printing Office, 1948.

U.S. Department of Defense. *Second Report of the Secretary of Defense for the Fiscal Year 1949.* Washington, D.C.: Government Printing Office, 1950.

————. *Semiannual Report of the Secretary of Defense.* For Periods Ending December 31, 1949; June 30, 1950; December 31, 1950; June 30, 1952; June 30, 1953; December 31, 1953; June 30, 1954; December 31, 1954; and June 30, 1955.

————. *Annual Report of the Secretary of Defense, July 1, 1959, to June 30, 1960.* Washington, D.C.: Government Printing Office, 1960.

————. *Annual Report for Fiscal Year 1962.* Washington, D.C.: Government Printing Office, 1963.

————. *Annual Report for Fiscal Year 1963.* Washington, D.C.: Government Printing Office, 1964.

————. *Annual Report of the Secretary of Defense on Reserve Forces, Fiscal Year 1963.* Washington, D.C.: December 20, 1963.

————. *Annual Report of the Secretary of Defense on Reserve Forces, Fiscal Year 1964.* Washington, D.C.: January 4, 1965.

U.S. House Committee on Appropriations. *Hearings, National Military Establishment Appropriation Bill for 1950.* Parts 1–4. 81st Cong., 1st sess., 1949.

————. *Department of Defense Appropriation Bill, 1959.* H. Rept. 1830 to accompany H.R. 12738. 85th Cong., 2d sess., 1958.

————. *Department of Defense Appropriation Bill, 1959.* H. Rept. 2503 (Conference Rept.) on H.R. 12738. 85th Cong., 2d sess., 1958.

————. *Hearings, Department of Defense Appropriations for 1959: Department of the Army.* 85th Cong., 2d sess., 1958.

————. *Hearings, Department of Defense Appropriations for 1959: Overall Policy Statements.* 85th Cong., 2d sess., 1958.

————. *Department of Defense Appropriation Bill, 1960.* H. Rept. 408 to accompany H.R. 7454. 86th Cong., 1st sess., 1959.

————. *Department of Defense Appropriation Bill, 1960.* H. Rept. 743 (Conference Rept.) on H.R. 7454. 86th Cong., 1st sess., 1959.

————. *Hearings, Department of Defense Appropriations for 1960: Manpower, Personnel, and Reserves.* Part 3. 86th Cong., 1st sess., 1959.

————. *Hearings, Department of Defense Appropriations for 1961.* Part 2. 86th Cong., 2d sess., 1960.

————. *Hearings, Department of Defense Appropriations for 1965: Military Personnel.* Part 1. 88th Cong., 2d sess., 1964.

U.S. House Committee on Armed Services. *Retirement of Regular Army Personnel and Personnel of the Reserve Components of All Services.* H. Rept. 816 to accompany H.R. 2744. 80th Cong., 1st sess., 1947.

————. *Subcommittee Hearings on H.R. 2744.* Committee Paper No. 169. 80th Cong., 1st sess., 1947.

————. *Armed Forces Reserve Act of 1951, The.* H. Rept. 1066 to accompany H.R. 5426. 82d Cong., 1st sess., 1951.

————. *Hearings, Reserve Components.* H.R. 4860. 82d Cong., 1st sess., 1951.

————. *Armed Forces Reserve Act of 1952.* H. Rept. 2445 (Conference Rept.) on H.R. 5426. 82d Cong., 2d sess., 1952.

————. *Hearings, Reserve Officer Personnel Act.* H.R. 1222. 83d Cong., 1st sess., 1953.

————. *Reserve Officer Personnel Act.* H. Rept. 1026 to accompany H.R. 6573. 83d Cong., 1st sess., 1953.

————. *Hearings, National Reserve Plan.* H.R. 2967. Committee Paper No. 11. 84th Cong., 1st sess., 1955.

————. *National Reserve Plan.* H. Rept. 457 to accompany H.R. 5297. 84th Cong., 1st sess., 1955.

————. *Providing for the Strengthening of the Reserve Forces.* H. Rept. 987 to accompany H.R. 7000. 84th Cong., 1st sess., 1955.

————. *Reserve Officer Personnel Act Amendments.* H. Rept. 904 to accompany S. 1718. 84th Cong., 1st sess., 1955.

————. *Subcommittee Hearings on H.R. 6900 and H.R. 7000.* Committee Paper No. 26. 84th Cong., 1st sess., 1955.

————. *Subcommittee Hearings on S. 1718.* Committee Paper No. 21. 84th Cong., 1st sess., 1955.

————. *Reserve Forces Legislation: A Legislative History of the Reserve Forces Act of 1955.* Committee Paper No. 82 prepared by Eileen Galloway. 84th Cong., 2d sess., 1956.

————. *Review of Reserve Program by Subcommittee No. 1.* Committee Paper No. 41, 84th Cong., 2d sess., 1956.

————. *Review of Reserve Program of Subcommittee No. 1, May, 1956.* Committee Paper No. 81, 84th Cong., 2d sess., 1956.

————. *History of United States Military Policy on Reserve Forces, 1775–1957.* Committee Paper No. 17 prepared by Eileen Galloway. 85th Cong., 1st sess., 1957.

————. *Review of the Reserve Program.* Committee Paper No. 22. 85th Cong., 1st sess., 1957.

————. *Review of Reserve Program by Subcommittee No. 1.* Committee Paper No. 35. 85th Cong., 1st sess., 1957.

————. *Expressing the Sense of the Congress with Respect to the Size of the Army National Guard.* H. Rept. 2199 to accompany H. Con. Res. 333. 85th Cong., 2d sess., 1958.

————. *Full Committee Consideration of Subcommittee No. 1 Resolutions Relating to National Guard and Reserves.* Committee Paper No. 74. 85th Cong., 2d sess., 1958.

————. *Hearings, Proposed Reduction in the Strength of the National Guard.* Committee Paper No. 77. 85th Cong., 2d sess., 1958.

————. *Hearings, Review of the Reserve Program.* Committee Paper No. 72. 86th Cong., 2d sess., 1960.

————. *Authorizing Appropriations for Aircraft, Missiles, and Naval Vessels.* H. Rept. 1406. 87th Cong., 2d sess., 1962.

————. *Military Reserve Posture Hearings.* Committee Paper No. 66. 87th Cong., 2d sess., 1962.

————. *Report of Subcommittee No. 3 on Military Reserve Posture.* Committee Paper No. 70, 87th Cong., 2d sess., 1962.

————. *Hearings Before Subcommittee No. 3 and Full Committee on H.R. 4241 and H.R. 6996.* Committee Paper No. 15. 88th Cong., 1st sess., 1963.

————. *Hearings, Reserve Officers' Training Corps Program.* H.R. 4427, H.R. 4444, H.R. 8130, and H.R. 9124. Committee Paper No. 33. 88th Cong., 1st sess., 1963.

————. *Reserve Officers' Training Corps Program.* H. Rept. 925 to accompany H.R. 9124. 88th Cong., 1st sess., 1963.

————. *Hearings on Military Posture and H.R. 9637.* Committee Paper No. 36. 88th Cong., 2d sess., 1964.

————. *Hearings, Merger of the Army Reserve Components.* Committee Paper No. 39. 89th Cong., 1st sess., 1965.

————. *Hearings on Military Posture and H.R. 4016.* Committee Paper No. 7. 89th Cong., 1st sess., 1965.

U.S. House Committee on Government Operations. *Replies from Executive Departments and Federal Agencies to Inquiry Regarding Use of Industry Advisory Committees.* Parts 4 and 5, Department of Defense. 84th Cong., 2d sess., 1956.

————. *Amending the Administrative Expenses Act of 1946, And for Other Reasons.* H. Rept. 576 to accompany H.R. 7390. 85th Cong., 1st sess., 1957.

U.S. House Committee on Military Affairs. *Hearings on H.R. 6954, H.R. 7063 and Other Bills Relating to Retirement.* 79th Cong., 2d sess., 1946.

U.S. House Judiciary Committee. *Hearings to Incorporate the Reserve Officers Association.* H.R. 10299. 70th Cong., 1st sess., 1928.

U.S. House of Representatives. *Military Security of the United States.* H. Doc. No. 68. Message from the President of the United States. 84th Cong., 1st sess., 1955.

U.S. National Military Establishment. *Reserve Forces for National Security.* Report to the Secretary of Defense by the Committee on Civilian Components, June 30, 1948.

U.S. Senate Committee on Appropriations. *Hearings, National Military Establishment Appropriation Bill for 1950.* H.R. 4146. 81st Cong., 1st sess., 1949.

————. *Department of Defense Appropriation Bill, 1959.* S. Rept. 1937 to accompany H.R. 12738. 85th Cong., 2d sess., 1958.

————. *Hearings, Department of Defense Appropriations for 1959.* H.R. 12738. 85th Cong., 2d sess., 1958.

————. *Department of Defense Appropriation Bill, 1960.* S. Rept. 476 to accompany H.R. 7454. 86th Cong., 1st sess., 1959.

————. *Hearings, Department of Defense Appropriations for 1960.* H.R. 7454. 86th Cong., 1st sess., 1959.

————. *Hearings, Department of Defense Appropriations for 1965: Military Personnel.* Part 2. H.R. 10939. 88th Cong., 2d sess., 1964.

U.S. Senate Committee on Armed Services. *Hearings, Army and Air Force Vitalization and Retirement Equalization Act of 1948.* H.R. 2744. 80th Cong., 2d sess., 1948.

————. *Providing for Elimination of Regular Army and Regular Air Force Officers.* S. Rept. 1543 to accompany H.R. 2744. 80th Cong., 2d sess., 1948.

————. *Armed Forces Reserve Act of 1952.* S. Rept. 1795 to accompany H.R. 5426. 82d Cong., 2d sess., 1952.

————. *Hearings, Armed Forces Reserve Act of 1952.* H.R. 5426. 82d Cong., 2d sess., 1952.

————. *Hearings, National Security Training Corps Act.* S. 2441. 82d Cong., 2d sess., 1952.

U.S. Senate Committee on Armed Services. *Hearings, Reserve Officer Personnel Act of 1954.* H.R. 6573. 83d Cong., 2d sess., 1954.

———. Interim Subcommittee on Preparedness. *Status of Reserve and National Guard Forces of the Armed Services.* Second Report. 83d Cong., 2d sess., 1954.

———. *Reserve Officer Personnel Act of 1954.* S. Rept. 2010 to accompany H.R. 6573. 83d Cong., 2d sess., 1954.

———. *Hearings, Amendments to the Reserve Officer Personnel Act of 1954.* S. 1718. 84th Cong., 1st sess., 1955.

———. *Hearings, National Reserve Plan.* H.R. 7000. 84th Cong., 1st sess., 1955.

———. *Providing for Strengthening of the Reserve Forces.* S. Rept. 840 to accompany H.R. 7000. 84th Cong., 1st sess., 1955.

———. *Reserve Officer Personnel Act Amendments.* S. Rept. 368 to accompany S. 1718. 84th Cong., 1st sess., 1955.

———. *Hearings, Major Defense Matters.* Part 2. 86th Cong., 1st sess., 1959.

———. *Hearings, ROTC Vitalization Act of 1964.* H.R. 9124. 88th Cong., 2d sess., 1964.

———. *ROTC Vitalization Act of 1964.* S. Rept. 1514 to accompany H.R. 9124. 88th Cong., 2d sess., 1964.

———. Preparedness Investigating Subcommittee. *Hearings, Proposal to Realine the Army National Guard and the Army Reserve Forces.* 89th Cong., 1st sess., 1965.

U.S. Senate Committee on Judiciary. *Reserve Officers Association of the United States.* S. Rept. 1913 to accompany H.R. 5002. 81st Cong., 2d sess.; 1950.

U.S. Senate Committee on Military Affairs. *Hearings, Retirement.* S. 1974. 79th Cong., 2d sess., 1946.

U.S. Treasury Department. *Annual Report of the Secretary of the Treasury on the State of the Finances for Fiscal Year Ended June 30, 1950.* Washington, D.C.: Government Printing Office, 1951.

———. *Combined Statement of Receipts, Expenditures and Balances of the U.S. Government for the Fiscal Year Ended June 30, 1963.*

———. Bureau of Accounts. *Combined Statement of Receipts, Expenditures and Balances of the United States Government for the Fiscal Year Ended June 30, 1964.*

UPTON, EMORY. *The Military Policy of the United States.* S. Doc. No. 494. 62d Cong., 2d sess., 1904. Washington, D.C.: Government Printing Office, 1904.

PROCEEDINGS

Mershon National Security Program. *Role of Colleges and Universities in ROTC Programs.* Ohio State University, June, 1960.

Official Proceedings of the National Guard Association of the United States. Annual Conventions and General Conferences, 1948–64.

Proceedings of the Regional ROTC Conference, Lehigh University, May 8–9, 1933. Washington, D.C.: Civilian Military Education Fund, 1933.

UNPUBLISHED MATERIALS

MORRILL, CHESTER. "Mission and Organization of the Army National Guard of the United States: With Emphasis on the Period since 1952." Unpublished Ph.D. dissertation, American University, 1958.

STORY, CHARLES DALE. "The Formulation of Army Reserve Forces Policy: Its Setting amidst Pressure Group Activity." Unpublished Ph.D. dissertation, University of Oklahoma, 1958.

INTERVIEWS

AILES, STEPHEN, former Secretary of the Army, October 12, 1965.

BENNETT, CHARLES E., Congressman, Florida, Member, House Armed Services Committee, October 12, 1965.

BOYER, COLONEL CHARLES M., Former Executive Director of the Reserve Officers Association, March 24, 1964.

BRACKETT, COLONEL ARTHUR A., Director of Air Force Affairs, Reserve Officers Association, March 26, 1964.

BRASSWELL, EDWARD, Member of Staff, Senate Armed Services Committee, October 13, 1965.

BRAY, WILLIAM G., Congressman, Indiana, Member, Committee on Armed Services, October 13, 1965.

CANTWELL, MAJOR GENERAL JAMES F., Chief of Staff, Department of Defense, State of New Jersey, and President, National Guard Association of the United States, May 22, 1964.

CARLTON, COLONEL JOHN T., Executive Director, Reserve Officers Association, March 23, 24, 27, and May 25, 26, and 29, 1964.

CLATINOFF, COLONEL WALTER G. W., Air Force Professor of Military Science and Tactics at Rutgers—The State University, May 22, 1964.

DONNELLY, CHARLES H., Senior Research Specialist in National Defense, Library of Congress, February 26, 1964.

FORD, JOHN, Congressional editor of *Army Times*, March 26, 1964.

FRANK, MAJOR GENERAL JAMES E., President of the Reserve Officers Association, 1963–64, March 31 and May 14, 1964.

GALLOWAY (MRS.), EILEEN, Research Specialist in National Defense, Library of Congress, February 25, 1964.

GALUSHA, BRIGADIER GENERAL MARK, Executive Director, National Guard Association, May 27, 1964.

HARLOW, BRYCE N., Former Presidential Assistant to President Dwight Eisenhower, May 27, 1964.

HÉBERT, F. EDWARD, Congressman, Louisiana, Chairman, Armed Services Subcommittee No. 2, October 13, 1965.

HECHLER, KEN, Congressman, West Virginia, March 26, 1964.

HEDBERG, L. EUGENE, Staff Director, Reserve Forces Policy Board, February 26 and March 27, 1964.

HOLLINGSWORTH, COLONEL J. D., Deputy Assistant Secretary of Defense for Reserve Affairs, May 28, 1964.

HUGHES, R. ADM. WILLIAM C., Assistant Chief for Naval Affairs, Bureau of Personnel, Department of the Navy, May 28, 1964.

JACKSON, R. ADM. ALEXANDER, Assistant Executive Director and Director of Naval Affairs, Reserve Officers Association, March 25, 1964.

KENAN, BRIGADIER GENERAL THOMAS A., Deputy Chief, Office of Reserve Components, Department of the Army, May 28, 1964.

LENNON, ALTON, Congressman, North Carolina, Member, Committee on Armed Services, October 13, 1965.

LODOEN, MAJOR GENERAL GEORGE O. N., Director of Army Affairs, Reserve Officers Association, March 24, 1964.

McDONALD, COLONEL EUGENE O., Army Professor of Military Science and Tactics at Rutgers—The State University, November 17, 1964.

NAYLER, LIEUTENANT COLONEL JOHN L., Office of Chief of Legislative Liaison, Office of the Secretary of the Army, March 26, 1964.

NEDZI, LUCIEN N., Congressman, Michigan, Member, House Armed Services Committee, February 25, 1964.

NICHOLS, CAPTAIN J. C., Office of Assistant Chief of Naval Operations for Naval Reserve, Department of the Navy, May 28, 1964.

PALLADINO, MAJOR GENERAL RALPH A., Military Executive, Reserve Forces Policy Board, February 27 and March 27, 1964.

PAWSON, MAJOR WILBUR A., Army ROTC Instructor at Rutgers— The State University, May 18, 1964.

PIRNIE, ALEXANDER, Congressman, New York, Member, Armed Services Committee, October 14, 1965.

PRIMERANO, CAPTAIN VINCENT A., Executive Committeeman, Navy Section, Reserve Officers Association, May 21, 1964.

SIKES, ROBERT L. F., Congressman, Florida, Chairman, Appropraitions Subcommittee on Military Construction, October 13, 1965.

SLATINSHEK, FRANK M., Counsel, House Armed Services Committee, March 25, 1964.

SMITH, MARGARET CHASE, Senator, Maine, Committee on Armed Services, October 14, 1965.

SNYDER, LIEUTENANT COLONEL PHILIP E., Personnel Division, Office of Chief of Army Reserve, Department of the Army, March 26, 1964.

TWOMEY, COLONEL THOMAS, Acting Deputy for Air Force Reserves and ROTC, Department of the Air Force, May 27, 1964.

OTHER SOURCES

A Proposed Senior Division Army ROTC Curriculum. Ohio State University: Mershon Center for Education in National Security, 1965.

Reserve Officers Association of the United States. *ROA President's Manual.* n.d. (current).

INDEX

INDEX

INDEX